Secrets of Salt-Free Cooking

Jeanne Jones

Medical Preface by Rene Bine, Jr., M.D.
Practical Preface by Eleanor Bine
Epilogue by Belding Scribner, M.D.
Drawings by Karen Okasaki Sasaki

101 Productions / San Francisco

TO MY EDITOR, SHARON SILVA

In Grateful Acknowledgment:
Lee Ann Jones for recipe preparation and testing
Taita Pearn, M.S., R.D. for technical advice and professional assistance
Viola Stroup for technical and editorial assistance
Audrey Geisel for culinary consultation

Also by Jeanne Jones

The Calculating Cook
A gourmet cookbook for diabetics and dieters

Diet for a Happy Heart
A low-cholesterol, low-saturated-fat, low-calorie cookbook

Fabulous Fiber Cookbook
Recipes high in fiber, low in calories for diabetics and dieters

Copyright © 1979 Jeanne Jones
Drawings copyright © 1979 Karen Okasaki Sasaki

Printed and bound in the United States of America.
Distributed to the book trade in the United States
by Charles Scribner's Sons, New York.

Published by 101 Productions
834 Mission Street
San Francisco, California 94103

Library of Congress Cataloging in Publication Data

Jones, Jeanne.
    Secrets of salt-free cooking.

    Bibliography: p.
    Includes index.
    1. Salt-free diet--Recipes.   I. Title.
RM237-8.J66   641.5'632   79-343
ISBN 0-89286-146-0
ISBN 0-89286-147-9 pbk.

contents

medical preface

In the United States, more than 29 million are afflicted with cardiovascular diseases, the diseases of the heart and blood vessels. The major diseases of this system are hypertension (high blood pressure), atherosclerosis (the production of cholesterol and fibrin deposits in the walls of the arteries), rheumatic diseases and congenital defects. These in turn are responsible for one million deaths each year. As an underlying cause, atherosclerosis contributes directly to heart attack and stroke claiming 850,000 of these lives. Hypertension, too, afflicting more than 24 million in the United States, is a major contributing factor to these heart attack and stroke deaths.

Several factors have been identified as contributing to an increased risk of heart attack and stroke. These factors include some we cannot change, such as heredity, sex, age and race, but also those we can do something about, such as cigarette smoking, high blood pressure, elevated blood cholesterol, diabetes and lack of exercise. Obesity, too, contributes greatly through its effect on blood cholesterol, blood pressure and diabetes.

Nutrition—what we eat—plays a pivotal role in all this through its basic effect on blood pressure, cholesterol, diabetes and obesity. Sodium is an important nutrient in our diet, but as with so many things, North Americans overuse it. It is *not* a case of "if a little is good for you, a lot will be better." We consume far too much salt, and it is time that the population realizes it and does something about it to prevent diseases, rather than wait until they are upon us.

The appetite for salt is an acquired one, developed from infancy when the mother's habits and tastes are foisted on the child and further fortified through the years as a result of social and dietary customs. A normal individual in a temperate climate, performing actively, needs less than 2,000 milligrams of sodium per day (one level teaspoon of table salt contains 2,200 milligrams of sodium). Needs increase somewhat in nursing mothers and obviously in cases where sweating is

5

considerable. However, since sweat contains less than 1,000 milligrams of sodium per liter (approximately one quart), in America more than 4,000 milligrams would rarely be required except under unusual circumstances of location, occupation and hot humid climate. Yet the standard American diet contains around 10,000 milligrams of sodium per day and it is commonly much more due to the intake of salted snack foods!

The idea that habitual high salt intake may initiate hypertension is a very old one. The earliest effective treatment of hypertension was the rice diet, which was very low in salt. The use of diuretics to eliminate salt is well established in modern therapy for hypertension. Data both from animal experiments and human studies now give strong support to this old hypothesis. A genetic factor is also very important in both man and animals. Thus, many are not susceptible to the hypertensive effect of excessive salt intake but others (some 20 percent of North Americans) are highly susceptible.

In the United States, hypertension is more common in soft-water areas and in high rainfall areas where we find increased sodium content in the water along with low levels of calcium and magnesium. This is also especially true in areas where there are high concentrations of sodium in drinking water. It is clear from animal experiments that chronic salt loading has a delayed effect. It does not cause high blood pressure immediately, but sets in motion an upward trend which eventually becomes irreversible and is no longer corrected merely by reducing salt intake.

Today, the treatment of hypertension can be effectively accomplished because of the potent drugs that are now available for physicians to prescribe. Many physicians and patients have, however, become lulled into feeling that with the drugs no limitation of sodium need be enforced. This is certainly not the case. The effectiveness of these drugs is definitely increased by a moderate sodium restriction (down to 2,000 milligrams daily or even to 1,000 milligrams). One must be particularly aware of this since the loss of salt produced by the diuretic anti-hypertensive drugs may otherwise prompt the patient to increase the intake of salt. In fact, data now suggests that treatment with diuretics may tend to increase salt hunger. Then, too, the other anti-hypertensive drugs, such as reserpine, methyldopa, and even occasionally propanalol, can cause sodium to be retained. Actually, then, depending on the individual response to the drug therapy, further sodium limitation may be indicated, perhaps down to the 1,000-milligram level daily.

Congestive heart failure occurs when damage to the heart muscle from atherosclerosis, hypertension, heart attack, rheumatic fever, birth defects, etc., has reduced the heart's pumping power well below its normal capacity and it fails to act properly as a pump both in pulling blood into the heart via the veins and pushing blood out to the body through the arteries. Some of the results are the pooling of blood in the lungs, liver and abdomen, and retention of salt and water in the extremities and other parts of the body with consequent loss of oxygen and nutrients to the organs supplied by the arteries.

In the treatment of congestive heart failure, digitalis and diuretic medications are the mainstays. Digitalis increases the strength and efficiency of the heart muscle contraction, i.e., the pumping mechanism, while the diuretics reduce the work load of the heart by reducing the abnormal retention of sodium and water by the body. These drugs themselves, of course, can create nutritional problems, primarily in regard to sodium and potassium, over and above those inherent in the congestive failure process itself.

The patient with acute congestive heart failure will necessarily be markedly restricted in sodium intake, generally to as low as 500 milligrams (1.3 grams of salt per day). Later, usually a level of 1,000 milligrams of sodium will be settled on.

Because of their long-acquired taste for salt, many people balk at even this restriction by not eating, causing more nutritional problems, and frequently higher levels of sodium with necessarily higher doses of diuretics may be allowed by their physicians. It would be most unwise, however, to go above the 2,000-milligram level of sodium per day in anyone who has or has had congestive failure, for the possible harmful effects of increasing the dosage of any of the diuretics would be greatly enhanced. Washing out of too much salt does occur more readily in elderly patients who are on marked dietary sodium restrictions and this must be watched for. This is manifested by weakness, lassitude, anorexia (lack of appetite), nausea, vomiting, mental confusion, abdominal cramps and aches in skeletal muscles. Unfortunately, these symptoms differ little from those of digitalis overdosage in this group of people.

Restriction of sodium to very low levels is not without its hazards for some other people, since it may produce excessively low blood pressures. But this generally occurs only as a result of very strict sodium restriction in combination with diuretic therapy in someone with a severely damaged and flabby heart muscle or with large veins in the lower extremities. In these people, the assumption of a standing position after a recumbant or sitting position may cause weakness or dizziness as a result of sudden lowering of blood pressure.

The biggest problem in diet acceptance and compliance is that of motivation. It is a problem of habit. Real success depends on breaking a habit pattern and establishing new ones despite social, cultural and advertising pressures to the contrary. Consider that you are working for a permanent change in eating habits rather than the idea of "going on a diet." It is unfortunate but true that most people think of their *future health* as being way down on the list of important things to consider.

The depression of 1932 and a lot of other things were blamed on poor President Herbert Hoover, but perhaps the most detrimental thing he did to our health was to lend his name at the end of World War I to the term "Hooverize," to finish everything on your plate. We must realize that when we eat a part becomes sewage and the rest may take a long time to get off one's carcass. If we don't eat it, it goes directly to sewage, so why stuff to finish all on the plate?

Jeanne Jones, in this book, has put together recipes and recommendations for a three-pronged attack against the commonest ills to which mankind, and particularly North Americans, are subject. She started out, beautifully motivated by her own medical problem, with the book

7

for diabetics, *The Calculating Cook,* omitting sucrose from her recipes. This was followed, again because of familial motivation, by *Diet For A Happy Heart,* a cookbook for the individual trying to lower blood cholesterol levels and thus aid in the prevention of the ravages of atherosclerotic cardiovascular disease, particularly of the coronary arteries supplying the heart with oxygen and other nutrients. This book incorporated the low-cholesterol, low-saturated-fat principles of the American Heart Association as well as keeping the sugar low. In the past, virtually all of the so-called cookbooks and diet books directed at these diseases have made no attempt to lower the sodium intake of the individual to whom it is directed. In fact, the reverse has been true in most, thus allowing hypertension and possibly congestive heart failure to be building up in many people. At last, after painstaking work and meticulous testing, and the motivation of close friends, *Jeanne has done it,* bringing to you the low-sugar, low-cholesterol, low-saturated fat, low-sodium book you and we have been waiting for.

Remember, the sodium restriction to less than 800 milligrams per day as outlined in this book is a prescription diet and the patients adhering to this require counselling and monitoring by their physicians.

RENE BINE, JR., M.D.
Vice President, American Heart Association, 1978-1979
Past President, California Heart Association
Past Chairman, Nutrition Committee, American Heart Association

practical preface

I have been on a sodium-restricted diet for 25 years. For many years I struggled to make low-sodium food taste good. I wanted to achieve this for two reasons: I love good-tasting food—a variety of foods—and I wanted the food to taste so good that it could be enjoyed by family and friends as well as myself. I succeeded, but not to the extent that Jeanne Jones, a master of creative cooking, and her cookbook will allow you to.

The first thing that I want to impress on you is that your health should be your most important concern. As you read on, you may feel that staying on your prescribed low-sodium diet is a nuisance. It is only a nuisance because it is new to you. After awhile it will be as familiar and simple as your former diet. Also, on rare occasions you may find a waiter or a friend that is not very cooperative. Don't let them intimidate you. It is your well-being that is at stake. For years I was on such a very, very low-sodium diet that I carried a Teflon frying pan (in a fancy bag) when I went to a restaurant. I couldn't take a chance that my meat or chicken would be put on a broiler that had had food cooked with salt on it.

If you are just starting a sodium-restricted diet, please understand one thing: It will take awhile for your taste buds to adjust to a whole new taste experience. After several months, if someone serves you two plates of food, one with salt and one without, I promise you that you will prefer the food cooked without salt. There are some foods that you will not be able to have and this you must accept, i.e., luncheon meats, corned meats, ham and hot dogs.

Twenty-five years ago, there were few low-sodium products available and those that were available were difficult to find, even in health food stores. I even ordered some things directly from the manufacturers. Today, because of the medical education programs throughout the United States, there is a realization of many of the harmful effects of sodium on our health, in particular in relation to hypertension. This has brought public demand for more low-sodium

9

products, which manufacturers have complied with. Most health food stores now carry unsalted potato chips, corn chips, pretzels, sardines, tomato paste, tomato catsup, mustard, cheese and many other items.

When shopping, always read the labels. If there is salt or some salted product (i.e., soy sauce) or any ingredient that says sodium, such as sodium benzoate, sodium citrate, sodium bicarbonate (baking soda), sodium cyclamate, sodium hydroxide, sodium sterate, sodium nitrate (saltpeter), monosodium glutamate, sodium chloride (table salt), in the ingredients, it is *not* for you. There are some exceptions. If any of these ingredients are used in unsalted, low-sodium products, the amount is usually very small. The amount of sodium in products labeled "low sodium" is printed on the label. Usually the sodium figures are given per 100 milligrams or per tablespoon, per teaspoon, etc. This is your guide as to how much of the product you can use and still remain on your prescribed amount of sodium per day. Some foods labeled "low sodium" are not really very low in sodium. For example, a small can (one small portion) of low-sodium ravioli has about 250 milligrams of sodium. Beware of water-packed items, as some have salt added. Be careful when buying herb mixtures (i.e., chili powder, lemon pepper, etc.) for the same reason. Check frozen vegetables for salt or preservatives that have salt in them. Also, don't waste sodium on water. Use distilled water at home for drinking and cooking. There are even attachments for your kitchen faucet available that will remove all sodium from your water.

RESTAURANT DINING

The first assumption you must make is that your waiter doesn't know anything about low-sodium diets. Except in restaurants where I am known, I explain that for medical reasons I cannot have food cooked with salt or anything that has salt in it. I also tell the waiter that I am sorry to have to ask for special things but I have no choice. Before going to a new restaurant, I call and check to see if they have the following: separate cruets of vinegar and oil and unsalted butter or margarine. If they don't have them I bring them with me. I usually take a cube of unsalted butter or margarine in case I order something sautéed. (I leave the butter or margarine in the freezer until I am ready to leave for the restaurant; this saves me from dealing with its becoming soft.) I bring salad dressing in a small bottle (herb bottle), and crackers or melba toast. The following will give you an idea of what information you must give your waiter.

Salad Tell the waiter that you can have lettuce and any fresh vegetable. Tell him not to put any canned or cooked vegetables on the salad and no cooked dried beans, seafood or croûtons. Ask for the cruets of vinegar and oil. I have had waiters tell me they have vinegar and oil dressings already mixed. Decline, as these always have salt added.

Meat, Fish or Poultry Ask to have it broiled with nothing on it (no salt or other seasoning) and make sure it has not been seasoned or marinated. Ask if the chicken is raw or if it has been precooked. Some restaurants precook chicken with salt and then put it under the broiler to brown when ordered.

Soup Pass on all soups, as they all have salt added.

Potatoes I usually order a baked potato and ask that they bring it to me *unopened*. Or, you can just tell them not to put anything on the potato. Before ordering French-fried potatoes, check to see if the oil has salt in it. If the waiter is not sure, don't order them. If there is no salt in the oil, be sure and tell the waiter that you do not want salt added to the potatoes after they are cooked.

Noodles Pass on these as they are cooked in salted water.

Rice Some restaurants steam or cook their rice without salt. Ask before you order it.

Rice Pilaf This is almost always cooked with salt.

Vegetables There are a great many restaurants that cook their vegetables ahead of time and warm them just before serving. These are cooked with salt. In these restaurants, you may not be able to have a vegetable at all. It is always worth asking if they can steam or boil a vegetable without salt in the water, and no butter or margarine or seasoning added during or after cooking. In restaurants that cook vegetables to order there is no problem—just give them the above directions.

Desserts About the only dessert you can have is fresh, frozen or canned fruit.

In restaurants where orders are written on a tag and taken to the cook without an explanation from the waiter, ask the waiter to write on the tag "No salt on anything!" If the waiter tells you that they don't put salt on the foods you have ordered, please ask him to write it on the tag anyway because it is very important that you do not have salt. I had a waiter insist that no salt was put on hamburger patties or French fries and he refused to write "No salt" on the tag. When the hamburger and French fries arrived, they had been salted. When I spoke to the manager and he checked with the cooks, he found that one out of five always puts salt on one or

both of these items. Do not be intimidated by "know-it-all waiters." If you receive food that has been salted, send it back.

Because I enjoy dining out, I have selected seven or eight restaurants where I know my instructions will be followed without making me feel as if I am imposing on them. At these restaurants they will cook chicken, fish, rabbit, etc. with fresh mushrooms, green onions, parsley, herbs and wine. They use either their unsalted butter or margarine or some that I have brought with me. They steam or sauté vegetables or broil tomato halves. It takes a while to acquaint yourself with such restaurants. After you return a few times they will remember you, and your problems with dining out will be over.

SPECIALTY RESTAURANTS

These are (almost) impossible: Mexican, Chinese, Japanese, Moroccan, Indian. I prefer doing this kind of cooking at home. Also, beware of fast-food restaurants as they are not programmed for changes in their menu.

DINING IN FRIENDS' HOMES

Many people do not know what has salt (sodium) in it or have the attitude "a little won't hurt." When I am invited to a friend's home for dinner I explain about my low-sodium diet. If they offer to cook my food without salt, I make sure that they know how to do it. I always offer to bring my own food and in many instances do just that. I ask what will be served to other guests and then bring a dinner as close to what they are having as possible. I pack it in containers in which the hostess can easily heat the food.

If the hostess does cook my dinner, I usually tell her that I will bring my own bread, margarine or butter and salad dressing. When invited to a dinner party in a hotel, restaurant, etc., I again explain to the hostess and ask her if she would be kind enough to check with the chef about the possibility of fixing my food without salt. If it is okay, I usually ask that they keep it simple so that errors are not apt to happen: lettuce and tomato salad; cruets of vinegar and oil; broiled steak, lamb chops, fish or chicken (no salt or seasoning of any kind); baked potato (plain—leave closed); steamed or boiled vegetables (no salt in water, no butter or seasoning on vegetables); fresh, frozen or canned fruit. Bring your own unsalted butter or margarine and low-sodium bread. If this is not possible, bring your own food.

COCKTAIL PARTIES AND RECEPTIONS

These are impossible to take food to or have it separately prepared for you as you are usually standing and moving about and cannot stay near your food. One does not usually spend more than an hour or so at these parties, so plan to eat later. I can remember several times taking low-sodium hors d'oeuvres to a dinner party of about 20 people, and before I knew it, they were all gone and nobody was aware that they were low-sodium. I got very few for myself.

TRAVELING

Airplanes When making your reservation, ask for low-sodium meals. They have all kinds of special diets available. Be sure to check when you arrive at the airport that your low-sodium food is on the plane. I had one experience where it was forgotten. I usually carry some cheese and crackers with me just in case this happens.

Hotels When making your reservation, ask if there is a refrigerator in your room. If there is not, ask if a small one can be put in your room. Explain that you are on a restricted diet and have to carry certain foods with you that must be refrigerated. If neither of the above is possible, ask that you be allowed to put your things in one of their kitchen refrigerators. I have never been refused and have traveled a great deal. Figure the number of meals you will be eating and then wrap unsalted butter or margarine in foil, the size appropriate for each meal. Put bread and/or crackers in plastic baggies for each meal. Cut cheese (if you are taking some) in pieces appropriate for your use. Wrap in foil. Only the cheese and butter or margarine needs to be refrigerated. Put them in a box marked with your name and room number. If you ask to have your low-sodium bread toasted, be sure to tell the waiter not to put butter on it. Also ask that they keep an eye on it after putting it in the toaster, as it looks like regular bread and another waiter may accidently take it. I had this happen to me once.

To transport foods from home to hotel, I carry them in a thermos bag. I put baggies of ice cubes on top and bottom of the food if it is a trip longer than an hour.

Jeanne Jones has shown the "way" to diabetics, to those on low-cholesterol, low-saturated-fat diets, and now to those of us on sodium-restricted diets. I am grateful to her for caring so much about others.

ELEANOR BINE

introduction

As everyone who has read my other books knows, I love to cook and to entertain. The results of the time and effort that have gone into this book have been so rewarding that I think it will open new horizons in both the preparation and enjoyment of food for everyone on a sodium-restricted diet. Since I have been working on this book, I am delighted to find that my friends actually seem to be enjoying the meals I serve them more than ever, and they are experiencing a whole new range of flavors always before buried in too much added salt or other high-sodium ingredients.

Unlike other restricted diets where portion control and the omission of certain foods from the diet are enough, a low-sodium diet requires a whole range of special recipes and ingredients specifically for sodium-restricted diets. Even water in some areas is high enough in sodium content that distilled water is recommended for both drinking and cooking.

The major difference in developing truly delicious recipes for a sodium-restricted diet versus all other modified diets is that salt is a basic taste for which there is no real substitute. We have taste buds on our tongues for only four basic tastes. Starting at the tip of the tongue and working back they are sweet, salt, sour and bitter. For this reason it is necessary to actually "fool" the taste buds into thinking that the flavor-heightening quality given by salt is present by over stimulating one of the other basic tastes. You are probably already familiar with many recipes that list "salt to taste" as the final ingredient: That is because other than the four basic tastes, all of the "tastes" are actually *smells*. You will quickly discover that salt-free cooking will add a whole new dimension and importance to your sense of smell. If you don't believe this, hold your nose the next time you are eating one of your favorite foods and you will find you do not *taste* it.

Leaving the salt out of recipes or not putting a salt shaker on the table, or both, is not the answer for a truly low-sodium diet. This diet is instead a whole new concept in cooking. From birth we are all so accustomed to actually having our food "hyped" with salt, the great dietary whitewash, that many of the subtle, delicate flavors are missed completely. Low-sodium cooking is not only a new approach to seasoning, but also a whole re-education of the palate.

I have become so fascinated with the concept of salt-free cooking that I am actually having more fun than ever before developing new recipes and modifying the classics. I have even included many recipes for basic items such as low-sodium crackers, English muffins, sauces and salad dressings that are difficult, if not impossible, to buy commercially.

It is also difficult to eat out in restaurants without taking at least some of your own food with you, such as low-sodium bread, unsalted butter or margarine and salad dressing. You can almost always order fish, poultry or meat broiled or baked without added salt, unsalted vegetables and salads without dressing. Learning to cope with sodium restriction and restaurant dining presents a challenge that can be both fun and exciting if met optimistically. You will find that the more you learn about a low-sodium diet the more easily you can order in restaurants.

Because I love to entertain, one of my primary objectives in writing this book is to provide you with recipes so delicious and unusual that you will be able to serve your friends exactly the same foods allowed on your diet program. You can have imaginative and beautiful dinner parties of all types and will be amazed by the constant compliments from your guests.

This book may even inspire still another French approach to healthier recipe modification— *la cuisine sans sel.*

the low-sodium diet program

Before we start discussing all of the recipe and menu modifications necessary for a sodium-restricted diet, I think it is important to know what sodium is, where it comes from and why it should be limited.

Sodium is a soft, waxy, silver-white metallic chemical element occurring in nature in combined form. When combined with chloride it becomes ordinary table salt, the kind you put in salt shakers. There are about 2,200 milligrams (2.2 grams) of sodium in one teaspoon of salt. Sodium chloride is also found in all foods of animal origin, such as fish, meat and poultry, eggs and dairy products. Sodium is found in varying amounts in fruits, vegetables and even in water. (The exact amounts of sodium present in serving portions of all foods can be found in the food portion lists beginning on page 19.)

In general, fruits have the lowest sodium content, while vegetables vary widely. Some which are very low in calories are high in sodium, so if you are counting calories as well as sodium, choose your vegetables with care. Fresh vegetables are always best when available. When buying fresh frozen or canned vegetables, always check the labels for added salt. The sodium content of local water supplies varies greatly from one area to another. Check with your local water district, and if there are more than 30 milligrams of sodium per quart, it is advisable to use distilled water for both drinking and cooking. Home water softeners may be great for your laundry or shampooing your hair, but they do add a great deal of sodium to the water and therefore the water should not be used for either drinking or cooking. Many non-prescription laxatives, cold remedies, tranquilizers and headache medications have high-sodium content and you should check with your doctor before using them.

Sodium is an essential mineral that is necessary in the right amounts for everyday good health. One of the major functions of sodium in the body is working with chlorine to regulate the pH (a value used to express relative acidity and alkalinity) of the body fluids. In a properly functioning body, this works by a mechanism of the kidneys whereby chlorine is excreted if the tendency is toward the acid side and sodium is excreted if the tendency is toward the alkaline. It also regulates muscle contractions and nerve irritability.

Most people take in a great deal more sodium than is needed for proper body function and the excess amount is excreted by the kidneys. When the body is unable to get rid of the extra sodium because of diseases of the heart, circulatory system and kidneys, the unnecessary large amounts of sodium are accumulated. When sodium accumulates in the body, fluid accumulates along with it. The result is fluid retention that causes edema, a swelling of the tissues. This is dangerous because it makes the heart work harder and causes the blood pressure to go up. When this condition occurs it is necessary to restrict the amount of sodium in your diet.

If this happens, your doctor will prescribe a low-sodium diet program for you to follow. The most frequently prescribed low-sodium diet is for 1,000 milligrams of sodium per day; however there are cases where the diet prescription is as low as 500 milligrams or less of sodium per day. A diet restriction this low is extremely difficult to follow and requires constant monitoring of foods and beverages consumed.

The Secret Seven-Day Low-Sodium Diet on page 28 is designed for less than 800 milligrams of sodium and approximately 1500 calories per day. If it is necessary for you to lower the amount of sodium and/or the number of calories, you can still use this diet program as a guide, making substitutions or omissions where necessary. The program can also be used as a menu guide for party planning.

My own theory in writing this book for low-sodium diets has been "never say 'never'" about any ingredients. Obviously there will be exceptions to this theory as there are to all rules, including salt and foods cured or processed with salt, such as ham, corned beef, pickles and sauerkraut, to name a few. By carefully calculating the milligrams of sodium present in foods, however, it is possible to occasionally have foods considered taboo in most sodium-restricted diets. This means if you are particularly fond of celery, artichokes, Parmesan cheese, Worcestershire sauce, or even clams, normally on the forbidden lists for low-sodium diets, you may use them sparingly, carefully calculating the total number of milligrams of sodium in order not to exceed your doctor's prescribed limitation. For this reason you will occasionally find ingredients in recipes in this book not found in other low-sodium cookbooks.

There are 1,000 milligrams in one gram. Labels on low-sodium food products show the number of milligrams per 100 grams, which is about one-half cup. Serving sizes vary for each item, but the milligrams per serving and the serving size are also shown. Also be aware that some diet foods you may find in the same section in your market are for sugar-restricted diets only. It is important to read the labels carefully for sodium content. The more you learn about the nutritional content of foods and about low-sodium cooking in general, the more fun you will have cooking, eating and entertaining—and the more you will be able to use your imagination in both developing new recipes and modifying old ones.

In my recipes I specifically call for corn oil margarine. Pure corn oil margarine is considered by doctors to be better for your health than some of the other mixed oil margarines and it also has a better flavor when heated. Use polyunsaturated oils for salad dressings and for cooking. I always specify corn oil because I prefer the taste and texture over safflower oil and it is practically as low in polyunsaturated fats. I always specify unsalted mayonnaise in recipes because regular commercial mayonnaise is very high in sodium. I would suggest, however, using the Unsalted Mayonnaise recipe in this book because I think you will like it better than any you can buy commercially.

The food lists starting on page 19 follow closely the *Exchange Lists for Meal Planning* published by the American Diabetes Association in 1976. Therefore, you have a great deal more nutritional information than just sodium about all of the foods listed. I have used these lists both for categorizing foods and for calculating the nutritional information and available calories for all of the recipes in this book because many people on sodium-restricted diets also need other nutritional information.

Although I am using the Diabetic Exchange Diet for the diet program in *Secrets of Salt-Free Cooking,* I have made three changes in terminology, which seem to be more easily understood by everyone. First, the term "exchange" is changed to "portion." Second, the food group usually called "bread exchange" is titled "starches," which better describes the entire food group. Third, the food group usually called "meat exchange" is titled "proteins," again because it better describes the entire category.

The diet is to be used in exactly the same way as the Exchange Diet is used. Your doctor tells you how many portions of each food group you may have each day and how many milligrams of sodium. You then may choose from each food group the portion you wish for the meals during that day. The variety is practically endless. All that is important is that you have the proper number of portions from each food group each day and the correct number of milligrams of sodium.

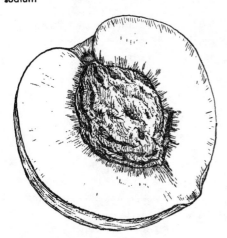

mg.
sodium = milligrams of sodium

FRUIT PORTION LIST

Each portion below equals 1 Fruit
Portion and contains approximately:
10 grams of carbohydrate
40 calories

* good source of Vitamin C
** good source of Vitamin A
*** good source of Vitamins
   A and C
†† sodium figures not available

mg.
sodium

1	Apple: 1 2 inches in diameter
.7	Apple juice: 1/3 cup
2	Applesauce, unsweetened: 1/2 cup
1	Apricots, fresh: 2 medium**
3	Apricots, dried: 3 halves**
	Avocado: see Fat Portion List
5	Banana: 1/2 small
1	Blackberries: 1/2 cup
1	Blueberries: 1/2 cup
10	Cantaloupe: 1/4 6 inches in diameter***

1	Cherries, sweet: 10 large
2	Cranberries, unsweetened: 1 cup
††	Crenshaw melon: 2-inch wedge
2	Dates: 2
2	Date "sugar": 1 tablespoon
1	Figs, fresh: 1 large
7	Figs, dried: 1 large
0	Fructose: 1 tablespoon
1	Grapefruit: 1/2 4 inches in diameter*
1	Grapefruit juice: 1/2 cup*
2	Grapes: 12 large
2	Grapes, Thompson Seedless: 20 grapes
1	Grape juice: 1/4 cup
2	Guava: 2/3*
1	Honey: 2 teaspoons
27	Honeydew melon: 1/4 5 inches in diameter
6	Kumquats: 2
1	Lemon juice: 1/2 cup
1	Lime juice: 1/2 cup
††	Loquats: 3
3	Litchi nuts, fresh: 3
3	Mango: 1/2 small**
18	Molasses, blackstrap: 1 tablespoon
8	Nectarine: 1 medium
1	Orange: 1 small*
1	Orange Juice: 1/2 cup*
3	Papaya: 1/3 medium*
16	Passionfruit: 1
††	Passionfruit juice: 1/3 cup
1	Peach: 1 medium
3	Pear: 1 small
3	Persimmon: 1/2 medium
1	Pineapple, fresh or canned without sugar: 1/2 cup
1	Pineapple juice: 1/3 cup
6	Plantain: 1/2 small
2	Plums: 2 medium

3	Pomegranate: 1 small
2	Prunes, fresh or dried: 2
5	Prune juice: 1/4 cup
6	Raisins: 2 tablespoons
1	Raspberries: 1/2 cup
1	Strawberries: 3/4 cup
0	Sucrose: 1 tablespoon
2	Tangerines: 1 large or 2 small
1.5	Watermelon: 3/4 cup

VEGETABLE PORTION LIST

Each portion below equals 1 Vegetable
Portion, is equal to 1 cup unless otherwise
specified, and contains approximately:
5 grams of carbohydrate
2 grams of protein
25 calories

* good source of Vitamin C
** good source of Vitamin A
*** good source of Vitamins A and C
† calories negligible when eaten raw
†† sodium figures not available

mg.
sodium

††	Alfalfa sprouts†
40	Artichoke, whole, base and ends of leaves (1 small)
1	Asparagus†
4	Bean sprouts†
40	Beets (1/2 cup)
37	Beet greens
8	Breadfruit (1/4 cup)
22	Broccoli***†
16	Brussels sprouts*
16	Cabbage*†
24	Carrots (medium), 1**
12	Cauliflower†
100	Celery†
100	Celery root (1/2 cup)

19

38 Chard†
12 Chayote
†† Chicory**†
42 Chilies†
16 Chives***†
†† Cilantro†
24 Collard*†
8 Cucumber†
40 Dandelion greens†
2 Eggplant
10 Endive†
10 Escarole**†
10 Garlic (1/4 cup)
3 Green beans: see String beans
8 Green onion tops†
†† Jerusalem artichokes (1/2 cup)
†† Jicama
94 Kale*†
12 Leeks (1/2 cup)
7 Lettuce†
.5 Lima beans, baby (1/4 cup)
†† Mint†
10 Mushrooms†
12 Mustard, fresh *†
4 Okra
9 Onions (1/2 cup)
†† Palm heart
32 Parsley ***†
trace Peas (1/4 cup)
trace Pea pods (1/2 cup)
20 Peppers, green and red*†
8 Pimiento (1/2 cup)
†† Poke†
2 Pumpkin (1/2 cup)*
20 Radishes†
2 Rhubarb†
4 Romaine lettuce†
4 Rutabagas (1/2 cup)
9 Shallots (1/2 cup)
37 Spinach†
1 Squash, acorn (1/2 cup)

1 Squash, Hubbard (1/2 cup)
2 Squash, spaghetti
6 String beans
2 Summer squash†
6 Tomatoes (1 medium)
15 Tomatoes, canned in juice, unsalted (1/2 cup)
282 Tomato catsup, regular (1-1/2 tablespoons)
6 Tomato catsup, dietetic, low-sodium (1-1/2 tablespoons)
244 Tomato juice (1/2 cup)
26 Tomato juice, unsalted (1/2 cup)
186 Tomato paste (2 tablespoons)
12 Tomato paste, unsalted (3 tablespoons)
831 Tomato sauce (1/2 cup)
42 Tomato sauce, unsalted (1/2 cup)
27 Turnips (1/2 cup)
550 V-8 juice (2/3 cup)**
49 V-8 juice, unsalted (2/3 cup)**
8 Water chestnuts (medium) (4)
16 Watercress**†
1 Zucchini squash†

STARCH PORTION LIST

Each portion below equals 1 Starch Portion and contains approximately:
15 grams of carbohydrate
2 grams of protein
70 calories

* good source of Vitamin A
†† sodium figures not available

mg. sodium	VEGETABLES
3	Beans, dried, cooked, unsalted (lima, soya, navy, pinto, kidney): 1/2 cup
1.5	Beans, baked, without salt or pork: 1/4 cup
1	Corn, on-the-cob: 1 4 inches long
1	Corn, cooked and drained: 1/3 cup
††	Hominy: 1/2 cup
14	Lentils, dried, cooked: 1/2 cup
8	Parsnips: 1 small
13	Peas, dried, cooked (black-eyed, split): 1/2 cup
7	Potatoes, sweet, yams: 1/4 cup**
2	Potatoes, white, baked or boiled: 1 2 inches in diameter
2	Potatoes, white, mashed: 1/2 cup
300	Potato chips: 15 2 inches in diameter
4	Pumpkin, canned: 1 cup
6	Rice, brown, cooked, unsalted: 1/3 cup
3	Rice, white, cooked, unsalted: 1/2 cup
4	Rice, wild, cooked, unsalted: 1/2 cup
564	Tomato catsup, commercial: 3 tablespoons
12	Tomato catsup, dietetic, low-sodium: 3 tablespoons

mg. sodium	BREADS
††	Bagel: 1/2
185	Biscuit: 1 2 inches in diameter
7	Bread, low sodium: 1 slice
139	Bread, rye: 1 slice
136	Bread, whole wheat: 1 slice
148	Bread (white and sourdough): 1 slice
200	Breadsticks: 4 7 inches long
116	Bun, hamburger: 1/2
153	Bun, hot dog: 2/3
245	Corn bread: 1 piece 1-1/2 inches square
††	Cracked wheat (bulgur): 1-1/2 tablespoons
140	Croûtons, plain: 1/2 cup
7	Croûtons, plain, low-sodium bread: 1/2 cup
133	English muffin: 1/2
1	Matzo cracker, plain: 1 6 inches in diameter
222	Melba toast: 6 slices
117	Muffin, unsweetened: 1 2 inches in diameter
412	Pancakes: 2 3 inches in diameter
7	Pancakes, low sodium: 2 3 inches in diameter
88	Popover: 1
143	Roll: 1 2 inches in diameter
70	Rusks: 2
712	Spoon bread: 1/2 cup
trace	Tortilla, corn, flour: 1 7 inches in diameter
203	Waffle: 1 4 inches in diameter

mg. sodium	CEREALS
287	All-Bran: 1/2 cup
94	Bran Flakes: 1/2 cup
††	Bran, unprocessed rice: 1/3 cup
††	Bran, unprocessed wheat: 1/3 cup
240	Cheerios: 1 cup
††	Concentrate: 1/4 cup
178	Corn Flakes: 2/3 cup
1	Cornmeal, cooked: 1/2 cup
1	Cream-of-Wheat, cooked: 1/2 cup
147	Grapenuts: 1/4 cup
113	Grapenut Flakes: 1/2 cup
1	Grits, cooked: 1/2 cup
165	Kix: 3/4 cup
132	Life: 1/2 cup
1	Malt-O-Meal, cooked: 1/2 cup
2	Maypo, cooked: 1/2 cup
1	Matzo meal, cooked: 1/2 cup
1	Oatmeal, cooked: 1/2 cup
92	Pep: 1/2 cup
1	Puffed rice: 1-1/2 cups

mg. sodium	FLOURS
2	Arrowroot: 2 tablespoons
1	All-purpose: 2-1/2 tablespoons
138	Bisquick: 1-1/2 tablespoons
††	Bran, unprocessed wheat: 5 tablespoons
1	Buckwheat: 3 tablespoons
1	Cake: 2-1/2 tablespoons
trace	Cornmeal: 3 tablespoons
trace	Cornstarch: 2 tablespoons
1	Matzo meal: 3 tablespoons
12	Potato flour: 2-1/2 tablespoons
1	Rye, dark: 4 tablespoons
1	Whole wheat: 3 tablespoons
1	Noodles, macaroni, spaghetti, cooked: 1/2 cup
2	Noodles, dry, egg: 3-1/2 ounces
1.5	Noodles, cooked, egg: 3-1/2 ounces

mg. sodium	CRACKERS
††	Animal: 8
33	Arrowroot: 3
††	Cheese tidbits: 1/2 cup
88	Graham: 2
10	Low sodium: 4
220	Oyster: 20 or 1/2 cup
90	Pretzels: 10 very thin, or 1 large
250	Saltines: 5, salted
69	Soda: 3, unsalted
192	Ritz: 6
225	RyKrisp: 3
130	Rye thins: 10
336	Triangle thins: 14
150	Triscuits: 5
††	Vegetable thins: 12
276	Wheat thins: 12

mg. sodium	MISCELLANEOUS
10	Cocoa, dry, unsweetened: 2-1/2 tablespoons
120	Fritos: 3/4 ounce or 1/2 cup
40	Ice cream, low-saturated fat: 1/2 cup
1	Popcorn, popped, unbuttered and unsalted: 1-1/2 cups

21

LOW-FAT PROTEIN PORTION LIST

Each portion below equals 1 Low-fat Protein Portion and contains approximately:

7 grams of protein
3 grams of fat
55 calories

†† sodium figures not available

CHEESE

mg. sodium	
234	Cottage cheese, low-fat: 1/4 cup
††	Cottage cheese, dry curd: 1/4 cup
222	Farmer's: 1/4 cup, crumbled, salted
75	Farmer's: 1/4 cup, crumbled, unsalted
††	Hoop: 1/4 cup
12	Pot: 1/4 cup
46	Ricotta, part skim: 1/4 cup or 2 ounces

EGG SUBSTITUTES

mg. sodium	
130	Liquid egg substitute: 1/4 cup (sodium content varies with brands)
††	Dry egg substitute: 3 tablespoons

CHICKEN

mg. sodium	
22	Broiled or roasted: 1 ounce or 1 slice 3 x 2 x 1/8 inches
19	Breast, without skin: 1/2 small, 1 ounce or 1/4 cup, chopped
25	Leg: 1/2 medium or 1 ounce

TURKEY

mg. sodium	
23	Meat, white, without skin: 1 ounce or 1 slice 3 x 2 x 1/8 inches
28	Meat, dark, without skin: 1 ounce or 1 slice 3 x 2 x 1/8 inches

OTHER POULTRY AND GAME

mg. sodium	
25	Buffalo: 1 ounce or 1 slice 3 x 2 x 1/8 inches
22	Cornish game hen, without skin: 1/4 bird or 1 ounce
20	Pheasant: 1-1/2 ounces
18	Rabbit: 1 ounce or 1 slice 3 x 2 x 1/8 inches
12	Quail, without skin: 1/4 bird or 1 ounce
22	Squab, without skin: 1/4 bird or 1 ounce
25	Venison, lean, roast or steak: 1 ounce or 1 slice 3 x 2 x 1/8 inches

FISH AND SEAFOOD

mg. sodium	
††	Abalone: 1-1/3 ounces
112	Albacore, canned in oil: 1 ounce
††	Anchovy fillets: 9
1540	Anchovy paste: 1 tablespoon
15	Bass: 1-1/2 ounces
624	Caviar: 1 ounce
51	Clams, fresh: 3 large or 1-1/2 ounces
††	Clams, canned: 1-1/2 ounces
††	Clam juice: 1-1/2 cups
31	Cod: 1 ounce
77	Crab, canned: 1/2 ounce
90	Crab, cracked, fresh: 1-1/2 ounces
110	Flounder: 1-2/3 ounces
††	Frog legs: 2 large or 3 ounces
30	Halibut: 1 ounce or 1 piece 2 x 2 x 1 inch
††	Herring, pickled: 1-1/4 ounces
2207	Herring, smoked: 1-1/4 ounces
90	Lobster, fresh: 1-1/2 ounces, 1/4 cup or 1/4 small lobster
90	Lobster, canned, unsalted: 1-1/2 ounces
31	Oysters, fresh: 3 medium or 1-1/2 ounces
171	Oysters, canned: 1-1/2 ounces
39	Perch: 1-1/2 ounces
38	Red snapper: 1-1/2 ounces
14	Salmon: 1 ounce
235	Salmon, canned: 1-1/2 ounces
33	Sand dabs: 1-1/2 ounces
108	Sardines: 4 small
26	Sardines, unsalted: 4 small
112	Scallops: 3 medium or 1-1/2 ounces
44	Sole: 1-2/3 ounces
60	Shrimp, fresh: 5 medium
††	Shrimp, canned: 5 medium or 1-1/2 ounces
††	Swordfish: 1-1/2 ounces
11	Trout: 1-1/2 ounces
10	Tuna, fresh: 1 ounce
370	Tuna, canned in oil: 1/4 cup
25	Tuna, unsalted, water packed (dietetic): 1/4 cup
32	Turbot: 1-1/2 ounces

BEEF

26 Flank steak: 1-1/2 ounces
17 Rib roast: 1 ounce, 1/4 cup, chopped, or 1 slice 3 x 2 x 1/8 inches
17 Steak, very lean (filet mignon, New York, sirloin, T-bone): 1 ounce or 1 slice 3 x 2 x 1/8 inches
21 Tripe: 1 ounce or 1 piece 5 x 2 inches

LAMB

mg. sodium

20 Chops, lean: 1/2 small chop or 1 ounce
20 Roast, lean: 1 ounce, 1 slice 3 x 2 x 1/8 inches, or 1/4 cup, chopped

PORK

mg. sodium

264 Ham: 1 ounce or 1 slice 3 x 2 x 1/8 inches

VEAL

mg. sodium

23 Chop: 1/2 small or 1 ounce
23 Cutlet: 1 ounce or 1 slice 3 x 2 x 1/8 inches
23 Roast: 1 ounce or 1 slice 3 x 2 x 1/8 inches

MEDIUM-FAT PROTEIN PORTION LIST

Each portion below equals 1 Medium-fat Protein Portion and contains approximately:
7 grams of protein
5 grams of fat
75 calories

†† sodium figures not available

CHEESE

mg. sodium

130 Cottage cheese, creamed: 1/4 cup
†† Feta: 1 ounce
227 Mozzarella: 1 ounce
163 Parmesan: 1/4 cup, 2/3 ounce or 4 tablespoons
46 Ricotta, regular: 1/4 cup or 2 ounces
247 Romano: 1/4 cup, 2/3 ounce or 4 tablespoons

EGGS

mg. sodium

59 Eggs, medium: 1
47 Egg white: 1
12 Egg yolk: 1

CHICKEN

mg. sodium

16 Gizzard: 1 ounce
20 Heart: 1 ounce
17 Liver: 1 ounce

BEEF

mg. sodium

54 Brains: 1 ounce
298 Corned beef, canned: 1 ounce or 1 slice 3 x 2 x 1/8 inches
14 Hamburger, very lean (4 ounces raw = 3 ounces cooked): 1 ounce
30 Heart: 1 ounce or 1 slice 3 x 2 x 1/8 inches
72 Kidney: 1 ounce or 1 slice 3 x 2 x 1/8 inches
59 Liver: 1 ounce or 1 slice 3 x 2 x 1/8 inches
17 Tongue: 1 slice 3 x 2 x 1/4 inches

PORK

mg. sodium

343 Canadian bacon: 1 slice 2-1/2 inches in diameter, 1/4 inch thick
18 Chops, lean: 1/2 small chop or 1 ounce
19 Heart: 1 ounce
30 Liver: 1 ounce
18 Roast, lean: 1 ounce, 1 slice 3 x 2 x 1/8 inches or 1/4 cup, chopped

VEAL

mg. sodium

30 Calves' liver: 1 ounce or 1 slice 3 x 2 x 1/8 inches
33 Sweetbreads: 1 ounce, 1/4 pair or 1/4 cup, chopped
22 Roast, lean: 1 ounce, 1/4 cup, chopped, or 1 slice 3 x 2 x 1/8 inches

HIGH-FAT PROTEIN PORTION LIST

Each portion below equals 1 High-fat
Protein Portion and contains
approximately:
7 grams of protein
7 grams of fat
95 calories

†† sodium figures not available

CHEESE

mg. sodium	
193	American: 1 ounce
510	Bleu: 1 ounce or 1/4 cup, crumbled
193	Cheddar: 1 ounce
10	Cheddar, low sodium: 1 ounce (sodium content varies with brands)
204	Edam: 1 ounce
271	Liederkranz: 1 ounce
204	Monterey Jack: 1 ounce
204	Muenster: 1 ounce
465	Pimiento cheese spread: 1 ounce
465	Roquefort: 1 ounce or 1/4 cup, crumbled
††	Stilton: 1 ounce or 1/4 cup, crumbled
85	Swiss: 1 ounce

COLD CUTS

mg. sodium	
266	Bologna: 1 ounce or 1 slice 4-1/2 inches in diameter, 1/8 inch thick
264	Liverwurst: 1 slice 3 inches in diameter, 1/4 inch thick
340	Spam: 1 ounce
425	Salami: 1 ounce or 1 slice 4 inches in diameter, 1/3 inch thick
228	Vienna sausage: 2-1/2 sausages or 1 ounce

DUCK

mg. sodium	
21	Roasted, without skin: 1 ounce or 1 slice 3 x 2 x 1/8 inches
28	Wild duck, without skin: 1 ounce

BEEF

mg. sodium	
17	Brisket: 1 ounce
508	Frankfurters: 1 (8 to 9 per pound)
18	Short ribs, very lean: 1 rib or 1 ounce

PEANUT BUTTER

mg. sodium	
156	Peanut butter, regular: 2 tablespoons
6	Peanut butter, unsalted: 2 tablespoons

PORK

mg. sodium	
	Bacon: see Fat Portion List
250	Sausage: 2 small or 1 ounce
19	Spareribs, without fat: meat from 3 medium or 1 ounce

FAT PORTION LIST

Each portion below equals 1 Fat
Portion and contains approximately:
5 grams of fat
45 calories

†† sodium figures not available

mg. sodium	
1	Avocado: 1/8 4 inches in diameter
209	Bacon, crisp: 1 slice
39	Butter: 1 teaspoon
.3	Butter, unsalted: 1 teaspoon
5	Caraway seeds: 2 tablespoons
5	Cardamom seeds: 2 tablespoons
4	Chocolate, bitter: 1/3 ounce or 1/3 square
35	Cream cheese: 1 tablespoon
12	Cream, light, coffee: 2 tablespoons
5	Cream, heavy, whipping: 1 tablespoon
18	Cream, half-and-half: 3 tablespoons
12	Cream, sour: 2 tablespoons
32	Cream, sour, imitation: 2 tablespoons (Imo, Matey)
35	Margarine, polyunsaturated: 1 teaspoon
.8	Margarine, polyunsaturated, unsalted: 1 teaspoon
25	Mayonnaise: 1 teaspoon
0	Oils, polyunsaturated: 1 teaspoon
125	Olives, ripe: 5 small
384	Olives, green: 4 medium
3	Poppy seeds: 1-1/2 tablespoons
††	Pumpkin seeds: 1-1/2 teaspoons

Salad dressings, commercial

59	Bleu cheese: 1 teaspoon
95	Bleu cheese, diet, sugar-free: 1 teaspoon
57	Caesar: 1 teaspoon
77	French: 1 teaspoon
74	Italian: 1 teaspoon
64	Italian, diet: 1 teaspoon
48	Roquefort: 1 teaspoon
44	Thousand island, diet: 1 teaspoon
33	Thousand island, egg-free: 1 teaspoon

Sauces, commercial

††	Béarnaise: 1 teaspoon
28	Hollandaise: 1 teaspoon
61	Tartar sauce: 1 teaspoon
4	Sesame seeds: 2 teaspoons
3	Sunflower seeds: 1-1/2 teaspoons

NUTS, UNSALTED

mg. sodium

.5	Almonds: 7
.5	Brazil nuts: 2
2	Cashews: 7
5	Coconut, fresh: 1 piece 1 x 1 x 3/8 inches
5	Coconut, shredded, unsweetened: 2 tablespoons
.5	Filberts: 5
.5	Hazelnuts: 5
††	Hickory nuts: 7 small
††	Macadamia nuts: 2
1	Peanuts, Spanish: 20
1	Peanuts, Virginia: 10
trace	Pecans: 6 halves
††	Pine nuts: 1 tablespoon
††	Pistachio nuts: 15
††	Soy nuts, toasted: 3 tablespoons
.5	Walnuts, black: 5 halves
.5	Walnuts, California: 5 halves

NON-FAT MILK PORTION LIST

Each portion below equals 1 Non-fat Milk Portion and contains approximately:
12 grams of carbohydrate
8 grams of protein
trace of fat
80 calories

mg. sodium

280	Buttermilk: 1 cup
155	Milk, powdered, skim, dry: 3 tablespoons
115	Milk, powdered, skim, mixed: 1/4 cup
6	Milk, powdered, low sodium (Featherweight): 3 tablespoons, dry, or 1 cup, mixed
127	Milk, skim, non-fat: 1 cup
121	Milk, skim, instant: 1 cup
165	Milk, evaporated, skim: 1/2 cup
75	Sherbet: 1 cup
116	Yogurt, plain, non-fat: 1 cup

LOW-FAT MILK PORTION LIST

Each portion below equals 1 Low-fat Milk Portion and contains approximately:
12 grams of carbohydrate
8 grams of protein
5 grams of fat
125 calories

mg. sodium

150	Milk, low-fat, 2% fat: 1 cup
12.5	Milk, Carnation Lo-Sodium Modified: 1 cup
115	Yogurt, plain, low-fat: 1 cup
141	Yogurt, flavored, low-fat: 1 cup

WHOLE MILK PORTION LIST

Each portion below equals 1 Whole Milk Portion and contains approximately:
12 grams of carbohydrate
8 grams of protein
10 grams of fat
170 calories

mg. sodium

136	Ice milk: 1 cup
120	Milk, whole: 1 cup
149	Milk, evaporated, whole: 1/2 cup
6	Milk, low-sodium Lonolac liquid: 1 cup
114	Yogurt, plain, whole: 1 cup

HERBS, SPICES, SEASONINGS, ETC.

Calories are negligible and need not be counted in the following list; however, many of these foods are extremely high in sodium and must be calculated very carefully.

mg. sodium

10 Bakon Yeast: 1 teaspoon (12 calories)
trace Bitters, Angostura: 1 teaspoon
425 Bouillon cube, beef (fat-free): 1 1/2-inch cube or 4 grams
10 Bouillon cube, beef (fat-free and salt-free): 1 1/2-inch cube or 4 grams

5 Bouillon cube, chicken (fat-free and salt-free): 1 1/2-inch cube or 4 grams
294 Chutney: 1 tablespoon (Crosset & Blackwell's Major Grey's)
1 Coffee: 1 cup
trace Extracts: 1 teaspoon
4 Gelatin, unsweetened: 1 envelope (1 scant table-spoon)
0 Liquid smoke: 1 teaspoon
63 Mustard, prepared: 1 teaspoon (French's)
811 Pickles: 1 2 ounce, without sugar
6 Rennet tablets: 1 ounce
2200 Salt: 1 teaspoon
2077 Soy sauce: 1 ounce (2 table-spoons)
6 Tabasco sauce: 1/4 teaspoon
trace Vinegar, cider: 1 tablespoon
5 Vinegar, red wine: 1 tablespoon
5 Vinegar, white wine: 1 table-spoon
58 Worcestershire sauce: 1 table-spoon (Lea & Perrins)

mg. sodium **HERBS AND SPICES**

2 Allspice, ground: 1 teaspoon
1 Allspice, whole: 1 teaspoon
trace Anise seed: 1 teaspoon
trace Basil: 1 teaspoon
trace Bay leaf, 1 leaf
4 Celery seed, ground: 1 teaspoon
2 Celery seed, whole: 1 teaspoon

31 Chili powder, seasoned: 1 teaspoon
trace Cinnamon, ground: 1 teaspoon
3 Cloves, ground: 1 teaspoon
1 Cloves, whole: 1 teaspoon
trace Coriander, ground: 1 teaspoon
trace Cumin seed: 1 teaspoon
1 Curry powder: 1 teaspoon
trace Dill seed: 1 teaspoon
trace Dill weed: 1 teaspoon
1 Fennel seed: 1 teaspoon
1 Garlic powder: 1 teaspoon
1 Ginger, ground: 1 teaspoon
trace Juniper berries: 1
trace Lemon peel, dried: 1 teaspoon
trace Lemon peei, fresh: 1 teaspoon
2 Mace, ground: 1 teaspoon
trace Marjoram, dried: 1 teaspoon
trace Mint, dried: 1 teaspoon
trace Mustard seed: 1 teaspoon
trace Nutmeg, ground: 1 teaspoon
2 Onion powder: 1 teaspoon
trace Oregano, dried: 1 teaspoon
1 Paprika, ground: 1 teaspoon
5 Parsley flakes: 1 teaspoon
trace Pepper, black: 1 teaspoon
trace Pepper, cayenne: 1 teaspoon
698 Pepper, lemon: 1 teaspoon (Durkee's)
trace Pepper, white: 1 teaspoon
trace Rosemary, dried: 1 teaspoon
trace Saffron, powdered: 1 teaspoon
trace Sage, dried: 1 teaspoon
trace Savory, dried: 1 teaspoon
trace Tarragon, dried: 1 teaspoon
trace Thyme, dried: 1 teaspoon
1 Turmeric, ground: 1 teaspoon

ALCOHOLIC BEVERAGES

Whether you are allowed alcoholic beverages in your diet should be decided between you and your doctor. There is no question that weight loss/maintenance is simplified greatly by not drinking, as liquor of all types is high in calories. Also, as you will notice by the figures given, many alcoholic beverages are also high in sodium.

A good way to think of a cocktail, highball or glass of wine is to visualize the drink as a slice of bread with a pat of butter on it. This image helps me more to refrain from having another drink than anything else does.

There is another problem with drinking on a restricted diet. Alcohol can lead to waiting too long before eating, eating too much or eating something forbidden on the diet. Most doctors, however, consider cooking with wines completely acceptable. Wine adds very little food value to each portion, and all the alcohol is cooked away before the food is eaten.

mg. sodium	
17	Ale, mild, 8 oz. = 98 C, 8 GC
8	Beer, 8 oz. = 114 C, 11 GC

WINES

mg. sodium	
3	Champagne, brut, 3 oz. = 75 C, 1 GC
3	Champagne, extra dry, 3 oz. = 87 C, 4 GC
4	Dubonnet, 3 oz. = 96 C, 7 GC
4	Dry Marsala, 3 oz. = 162 C, 18 GC
4	Sweet Marsala, 3 oz. = 182 C, 23 GC
4	Muscatel, 4 oz. = 158 C, 14 GC
4	Port, 4 oz. = 158 C, 14 GC
4	Red wine, dry, 3 oz. = 69 C, under 1 GC
4	Sake, 3 oz. = 75 C, 6 GC
4	Sherry, domestic, 3-1/2 oz. = 84 C, 5 GC
4	Dry vermouth, 3-1/2 oz. = 105 C, 1 GC
4	Sweet vermouth, 3-1/2 oz. = 167 C, 12 GC
4	White wine, dry, 3 oz. = 74 C, under 1 GC

LIQUEURS AND CORDIALS

mg. sodium	
2	Amaretto, 1 oz. = 112 C, 13 GC
2	Crème de Cacao, 1 oz. = 101 C, 12 GC
2	Crème de Menthe, 1 oz. = 112 C, 13 GC
2	Curaçao, 1 oz. = 100 C, 9 GC
2	Drambuie, 1 oz. = 110 C, 11 GC
2	Tia Maria, 1 oz. = 113 C, 9 GC

SPIRITS

Bourbon, brandy, Cognac, Canadian whiskey, gin, rye, rum, scotch, tequila and vodka are all carbohydrate free! The calories they contain depend upon the proof.

mg. sodium	
trace	80 proof, 1 oz. = 67 C
trace	84 proof, 1 oz. = 70 C
trace	90 proof, 1 oz. = 75 C
trace	94 proof, 1 oz. = 78 C
trace	97 proof, 1 oz. = 81 C
trace	100 proof, 1 oz. = 83 C

C = calories
GC = grams of carbohydrates

secret seven-day low-sodium diet

The Secret Seven-Day Low-Sodium Diet offers menu plans for approximately 1500 calories per day day and less than 800 milligrams of sodium per day. Of course, all of the menus can be used for all calorie and sodium levels by slight additions or deletions. To calculate your own sodium levels in recipes, add up all of the milligrams of sodium in all ingredients and divide by the number of servings you are making.

All sodium figures in these menus are given for regular milk. It is possible to reduce the sodium substantially by replacing it with low-sodium milk.

DAY & TOTALS	BREAKFAST	LUNCH	DINNER
1 585 mg. sodium 1490 calories	1/2 cup fresh orange juice 1 soft-boiled egg 1-1/2 slices low-sodium bread, toasted, with 2 teaspoons unsalted butter or corn oil margarine 1 cup non-fat milk Coffee or tea **1 medium-fat protein portion** **1 fruit portion** **1-1/2 starch portions** **2 fat portions** **1 non-fat milk portion** **390 calories** **199 mg. sodium**	1 serving East Indian Tuna Salad 1 Giant Cinnamon Popover 1 cup low-fat milk Coffee or tea **1-1/2 low-fat protein portions** **1-1/2 fruit portions** **1 starch portion** **2-1/2 fat portions** **1 low-fat milk portion** **451 calories** **245 mg. sodium**	1 serving Cold Blueberry Soup 3 servings Roast Turkey, white meat 1 serving Southern Yam Casserole 1 serving Vegetarian Turkey Dressing 1 serving Perfect Pumpkin Pie Coffee or tea **3 low-fat protein portions** **3/4 medium-fat protein portion** **3-1/2 fruit portions** **2-1/4 starch portions** **1-1/2 vegetable portions** **2 fat portions** **649 calories** **141 mg. sodium**

DAY & TOTALS	BREAKFAST	LUNCH	DINNER

2
662 mg. sodium
 	
1466 calories
	1/2 cup Instant Cottage Cheese
	1/2 cup Overnight Oatmeal
	1 cup low-fat milk
	Coffee or tea
	
	1 low-fat protein portion
	1 fruit portion
	1 starch portion
	1 low-fat milk portion
	1/2 fat portion
	313 calories
	181 mg. sodium
		1 serving tossed green salad, with
		1 tablespoon Secret Italian
		   Dressing
		2 servings Turkey Cannelloni
		1/2 cup Low-Cholesterol
		   Zabaglione, over
		1/2 cup sliced fresh peaches
		Coffee or tea
		
		2-1/2 low-fat protein portions
		1-3/4 fruit portions
		2 starch portions
		1 vegetable portion
		4 fat portions
		1-1/4 low-fat milk portions
		709 calories
		188 mg. sodium
			1 serving Shades of Green Salad
			2 ounces Poached Salmon, with
			2 tablespoons Dill Sauce
			2 slices Dill Bread
			1 serving Savory Tomatoes Au
			   Gratin
			1 serving Cold Orange Soufflé
			Coffee or tea
			
			2-1/2 low-fat protein portions
			1/4 high-fat protein portion
			1-1/4 fruit portions
			2 starch portions
			3/4 vegetable portion
			1-1/2 fat portions
			441 calories
			293 mg. sodium

3
605 mg. sodium
 	
1570 calories
	1/4 cantaloupe
	1 ounce low-sodium cheddar
	   cheese, melted on
	1 English Muffin (2 halves), with
	2 teaspoons unsalted butter or
	   corn oil margarine
	1 cup non-fat milk
	Coffee or tea
	
	1 high-fat protein portion
	1 fruit portion
	2 starch portions
	2 fat portions
	1 non-fat milk portion
	445 calories
	154 mg. sodium
		1 serving Chinese Snow Pea Salad
		1 Pineapple Muffin
		1 cup low-fat plain yogurt
		Coffee or tea
		
		1-1/2 low-fat protein portions
		1 fruit portion
		1 starch portion
		1-1/2 vegetable portions
		2 fat portions
		1 low-fat milk portion
		446 calories
		191 mg. sodium
			1 serving Stracciatella alla Romana
			1 serving Italian Eggplant
			   Antipasto
			2 servings Gnocchi
			1 serving Osso Buco
			1 serving Amaretto Peaches
			Coffee or tea
			
			3-1/2 medium-fat protein portions
			1/2 high-fat protein portion
			1-1/2 fruit portions
			1-1/2 starch portions
			3-1/2 vegetable portions
			2-1/2 fat portions
			679 calories
			260 mg. sodium

DAY & TOTALS	BREAKFAST	LUNCH	DINNER
4 430 mg. sodium 1647 calories	1 banana, sliced, on 1-1/2 cups puffed rice cereal, with 1 serving Egg-and-Milk Cereal Topping Coffee or tea **1 medium-fat protein portion** **2-1/4 fruit portions** **1 starch portion** **1 low-fat milk portion** **360 calories** **74 mg. sodium**	1 serving Minestrone 1 serving Vegetarian Chef's Salad 1 slice Zucchini Bread 1 cup non-fat milk Coffee or tea **1/4 medium-fat protein portion** **1 high-fat protein portion** **2-3/4 starch portions** **1-1/2 vegetable portions** **5-3/4 fat portions** **1 non-fat milk portion** **684 calories** **204 mg. sodium**	1 serving Mystery Slaw 2 servings Game Hens Orangerie 1 serving Wild Rice à l'Orange 1 serving Zucchini in Basil Butter 1 serving Strawberries Hoffmann-La Roche Coffee or tea **4 low-fat protein portions** **2 fruit portions** **2 starch portions** **2 vegetable portions** **2-1/2 fat portions** **603 calories** **152 mg. sodium**
5 756 mg. sodium 1448 calories	1 Whole Wheat Waffle, with 2 teaspoons unsalted butter or corn oil margarine, and 1 tablespoon Honey Butter 1-1/2 Low-Sodium Sausage patties 1 cup non-fat milk Coffee or tea **3 medium-fat protein portions** **1 fruit portion** **2-1/2 starch portions** **2-1/2 fat portions** **1 non-fat milk portion** **633 calories** **226 mg. sodium**	1 serving Curried Orange Appetizer 1 serving Cottage Cheese Crêpes 1/2 cup Fast Frozen Yogurt 3/4 cup low-fat milk Coffee or tea **1-1/2 medium-fat protein portions** **1-1/2 fruit portions** **3/4 starch portion** **1 fat portion** **1 low-fat milk portion** **397 calories** **388 mg. sodium**	1 serving Gazpacho, with 6 Toasted Tortilla Triangles 1 serving Pisces Mexicana 1 serving Portuguese Pilaf 1 serving Bananas North Pole Coffee or tea **2 low-fat protein portions** **1-1/2 fruit portions** **2 starch portions** **2-1/2 vegetable portions** **1 fat portion** **418 calories** **142 mg. sodium**

DAY & TOTALS	BREAKFAST	LUNCH	DINNER
6 622 mg. sodium 1423 calories	1/2 cup Fruity Granola, mixed with 1/4 cup diced unsalted farmer's cheese, with 1 cup non-fat milk Coffee or tea **1 low-fat protein portion** **1-1/2 fruit portions** **1 starch portion** **1 fat portion** **1 non-fat milk portion** **310 calories** **210 mg. sodium**	1 serving tossed green salad, with 1/4 cup Fiesta Dressing 1 serving Baked French Onion Soup 1 slice French Bread, toasted 1 serving Cinnamon-Lemon Cheesecake 1 cup non-fat milk Coffee or tea **1 high-fat protein portion** **3/4 low-fat protein portion** **1/2 fruit portion** **2 starch portions** **1-1/2 vegetable portions** **2 fat portions** **1 non-fat milk portion** **508 calories** **273 mg. sodium**	1 serving St. Patrick's Day Potato Salad 1 serving Irish Stew 1 slice Irish Soda Bread 1 serving Poached Pears Coffee or tea **3 low-fat protein portions** **1-1/2 fruit portions** **2 starch portions** **3-1/4 vegetable portions** **3-1/2 fat portions** **605 calories** **132 mg. sodium**
7 562 mg. sodium 1483 calories	2 servings (slices) French Toast, with 1/2 cup Banana Cream Dressing 1/2 cup non-fat milk Coffee or tea **1 medium-fat protein portion** **3/4 fruit portion** **2 starch portions** **1 fat portion** **1/2 non-fat milk portion** **1/2 low-fat milk portion** **393 calories** **186 mg. sodium**	1 serving Curry Condiment Salad, on 1 cup cold cooked white rice 2 tablespoons Major Jones Chutney 1/3 medium papaya 1 cup non-fat milk Coffee or tea **3/4 medium-fat protein portion** **2-1/2 fruit portions** **2 starch portions** **1-1/2 fat portions** **1 non-fat milk portion** **444 calories** **194 mg. sodium**	1 serving Wilted Spanish Salad 1 serving Paella 1 serving Blueberry Mousse Coffee or tea **4 low-fat protein portions** **1-3/4 fruit portions** **1 starch portion** **2 vegetable portions** **5-1/4 fat portions** **646 calories** **182 mg. sodium**

stocks, bouillons and consommés

In a low-sodium diet, it is important to make your own stocks not only for better flavor, but also to achieve good flavor without high-sodium content. Though there are commercial low-sodium stocks, bouillons and consommés available, they are difficult to find and are often rather tasteless. You will also find that once you make your own stocks, not only will your soups and sauces be more delicious, but they will also be far less expensive.

If when you make your stocks they still seem too weak in flavor, boil them down to evaporate more of the liquid and to concentrate the strength. I routinely do this because a stronger flavor is essential in low-sodium cooking.

UNSALTED BEEF STOCK

4 pounds beef or veal bones
3 large onions, cut into quarters
2 carrots, scraped and sliced
6 garlic buds
4 sprigs parsley
2 whole cloves
1 teaspoon celery seeds
1 teaspoon dried thyme, crushed
1 teaspoon dried marjoram, crushed
2 bay leaves

1/4 teaspoon peppercorns
1-1/2 cups unsalted tomato juice
  (1 12-ounce can)
Defatted beef drippings, page 45 (optional)
Distilled water

Makes about 2-1/2 quarts (10 cups)
1 cup contains approximately:
Calories negligible when defatted
10 mg. sodium

Preheat the oven to 400°. Brown the bones for 30 minutes in a roasting pan. Add the onions, carrots and garlic and brown together for another 30 minutes, or until a rich, deep brown in color. Put the browned meat and vegetables in a large pot or soup kettle with all the remaining ingredients, adding the distilled water to cover by 1 inch. Bring slowly to a boil, then lower heat and simmer slowly for 5 minutes; remove any froth that forms on the surface. Cover, leaving the lid ajar about 1 inch to allow the steam to escape, and simmer slowly for at least 5 hours. (Ten hours are even better if you will be around to turn off the heat.)

When the stock has finished cooking, cool to room temperature. Refrigerate the stock, uncovered, overnight. When the fat has hardened on the surface, remove and discard it. Return the stock to the stove top and heat it just until it becomes liquid. Strain the liquid and taste it. If the flavor of the stock is too weak, boil it down to evaporate more of the liquid and concentrate its strength. Pour the stock into convenient-size containers and store in the freezer. You can then easily defrost only the amount of stock you need.

UNSALTED CHICKEN STOCK

3 pounds chicken parts (wings, backs, etc.)
1 whole stewing chicken (optional)
2 carrots, scraped and sliced
3 onions, cut into quarters
5 garlic buds
2 sprigs parsley
2 bay leaves
1 teaspoon dried basil, crushed

1/4 teaspoon peppercorns
Distilled water

Makes about 2-1/2 quarts (10 cups)
1 cup contains approximately:
Calories negligible when defatted
10 mg. sodium

Put the chicken parts, whole chicken (if using) and all remaining ingredients in a large pot or soup kettle, adding distilled water to cover by 1 inch. Bring slowly to a boil. Cover, leaving lid ajar about 1 inch to allow steam to escape. Simmer very slowly for 3 hours, or until whole chicken is tender. Remove chicken and continue to simmer stock for 3 to 4 hours. (If you are not cooking the whole chicken, simply simmer for 6 to 7 hours.) Cool stock to room temperature and proceed as directed for Unsalted Beef Stock, page 33.

Cooking the stewing chicken is helpful in two ways: First, it adds flavor to the stock. Second, it gives you a beautifully seasoned chicken for your dinner or chicken meat for preparing many other dishes, such as soups, sandwiches, etc.

UNSALTED TURKEY STOCK

1 turkey carcass
3 onions, cut into quarters
2 carrots, scraped and sliced
5 garlic buds
2 bay leaves
2 teaspoons dried basil, crushed
1 teaspoon dried thyme, crushed
1 teaspoon dried marjoram, crushed

1/4 teaspoon peppercorns
Defatted turkey drippings, page 45 (optional)
Distilled water

Makes 1-1/2 to 2 quarts (6 to 8 cups)
1 cup contains approximately:
Calories negligible when defatted
10 mg. sodium

Break up the turkey carcass and put it in a large pot or soup kettle. Add all remaining ingredients, adding the distilled water to cover by 1 inch. Cover, leaving the lid ajar about 1 inch to allow the steam to escape. Simmer slowly for 4 to 8 hours (depending upon how much time you have to watch the stock). Cool to room temperature and proceed as directed for Unsalted Beef Stock, page 33.

UNSALTED FISH STOCK

2 pounds fish heads, bones and trimmings
2-1/2 quarts distilled water
3 onions, sliced
6 sprigs parsley
1 carrot, scraped and sliced
1 teaspoon dried marjoram, crushed
1/4 teaspoon peppercorns

1/4 cup fresh lemon juice

Makes about 2 quarts (8 cups)
1 cup contains approximately:
Calories negligible
10 mg. sodium

Bring all ingredients to a boil in a large saucepan or soup kettle. Reduce heat and simmer, uncovered, for 45 minutes. Line a colander or strainer with damp cheesecloth and strain the fish stock through it. Cool to room temperature and store refrigerated up to 2 days or freeze.

UNSALTED COURT BOUILLON

1-1/2 quarts distilled water
2 cups dry white wine
1 lemon, sliced (with peel)
1 carrot, scraped and sliced
1 onion, sliced
2 garlic buds, cut in half
2 bay leaves

1/2 teaspoon celery seeds
1/4 teaspoon peppercorns
2 tablespoons fresh lemon juice

Makes about 2 quarts (8 cups)
Calories and sodium negligible because
        used only as a poaching liquid

Combine all ingredients in a large saucepan or soup kettle and bring to a boil. Reduce heat and simmer, uncovered, for 45 minutes. Strain and use for cooking shrimp, crab or lobster or for poaching any fish.

This court bouillon can be made ahead of time and used many times. Just strain after each use and store in the freezer. Of course, you can use fish stock for poaching fish, but this court bouillon is easier to make and completely satisfactory. A word of warning: Be careful not to overcook your seafood, or it will be tough. For example, when cooking shrimp never allow them to boil more than 2 minutes, then cool them in the court bouillon.

UNSALTED BEEF OR CHICKEN BOUILLON

1 part Unsalted Beef Stock, page 33, or
   Unsalted Chicken Stock, page 34
1 part distilled water

1 cup contains approximately:
Calories negligible
5 mg. sodium

Put the stock and water in a pan and bring to a boil. Simmer for at least 15 minutes before using.
   Basically, bouillons are just weak stocks. For this reason I find it troublesome and confusing to make both stocks and bouillons from scratch. It is troublesome because I think the bouillon made from a good, rich stock has a better flavor than most other bouillons, and confusing because I have enough trouble keeping track of everything in my freezer as it is. Use bouillon for cooking vegetables; it adds a lot of flavor and no food value.

UNSALTED BEEF CONSOMMÉ

2 egg whites
1 quart (4 cups) Unsalted Beef Stock, page 33
2 teaspoons dried chervil, crushed
2 sprigs parsley
1 cup chopped green onion tops

Freshly ground black pepper to taste

Makes 1 quart (4 cups)
1 cup contains approximately:
Calories negligible
10 mg. sodium

Whether serving consommé hot or cold, you will want it beautifully clear, and egg whites clarify it. Beat the egg whites with a wire whisk until they are slightly foamy. Add 1 cup of the cold stock to the egg whites and beat together lightly. Put the other 3 cups of stock in a very clean saucepan with all remaining ingredients. (It is not necessary to add all the seasonings, but the consommé will have a much better flavor if you do.) Bring the stock to a boil and remove from the heat. Slowly pour the egg white and stock mixture into the stock, stirring with a wire whisk as you do. Put the saucepan back on very low heat and stir gently until it starts to simmer. Put the pan half on the heat and half off so that it is barely simmering, then turning the pan around every few minutes, simmer for 40 minutes. Line a colander or a strainer with 2 or 3 layers of damp cheesecloth. Pour the consommé through the cheesecloth, allowing it to drain, undisturbed, until it has all seeped through. Then store until ready to use.

UNSALTED CHICKEN CONSOMMÉ

2 egg whites
1 quart (4 cups) Unsalted Chicken Stock,
    page 34
3 bay leaves
2 sprigs parsley
1 cup chopped green onion tops

White pepper to taste

Makes 1 quart (4 cups)
1 cup contains approximately:
Calories negligible
10 mg. sodium

Proceed exactly as for Unsalted Beef Consommé, preceding.

UNSALTED CONSOMMÉ MADRILENE

2 large ripe tomatoes, sliced
2 leeks, white part only, chopped
2 onions, sliced
1 carrot, scraped and sliced
2 tablespoons fresh lemon juice
1/4 teaspoon peppercorns
2 quarts (8 cups) Unsalted Chicken Stock,
    page 34
3 bay leaves

2 envelopes (2 scant tablespoons) unflavored
    gelatin
1/4 cup cold water
Freshly ground black pepper to taste

Makes about 1-1/2 quarts (6 cups)
1 cup contains approximately:
1 vegetable portion
25 calories
31 mg. sodium

Place vegetables, lemon juice, peppercorns, stock and bay leaves in a large pot or soup kettle. Bring to a boil, reduce heat to low and cover, leaving the lid ajar about 1 inch to allow steam to escape. Simmer for 2 hours.

Soften the gelatin in the water. Add gelatin mixture to hot consommé and stir until completely dissolved. Cool slightly and strain through a fine strainer. Add pepper to taste. Cool to room temperature, pour into a 1-1/2-quart mold and refrigerate. When the consommé is completely jelled, unmold by loosening the edges with the tip of a sharp knife, dipping the mold up to the rim in hot water for a *few seconds* and inverting onto a plate. Cut off the part containing the sediment and discard. Cut up the clear part and serve in sherbet glasses or cups.

soups

The variety of soups is almost limitless and this chapter reflects that. They can be served steaming hot, directly from the oven, such as the Baked French Onion Soup, or very cold, placed in icers, such as the Gazpacho. Soups are also a versatile part of the menu. They can be a light first course with practically no calories, such as Stracciatella alla Romana, or a hearty combination of ingredients suitable for an entrée, such as Sopa de Albondigas. Most importantly, they can be both flavorful and low in sodium.

COLD BLUEBERRY SOUP

3 cups fresh or unsweetened frozen blueberries
1 cup unsweetened pineapple juice
1 teaspoon fresh lemon juice
1/2 teaspoon vanilla extract
4 teaspoons low-fat plain yogurt

Makes 4 servings
Each serving contains approximately:
2-1/4 fruit portions
90 calories
5 mg. sodium

Put 2 cups of the blueberries, the pineapple and lemon juices and the vanilla extract in a blender container and blend until smooth. Divide the mixture into 4 chilled bowls, preferably set in icers to keep the soup very cold. (The soup also looks very pretty served this way.) Stir 1/4 cup of the remaining blueberries into each bowl and garnish each serving with a teaspoon of yogurt.

GAZPACHO

2 16-ounce cans unsalted tomatoes
1 medium onion, chopped
1 small green bell pepper, seeded and chopped
1 small cucumber, peeled and chopped
2 garlic buds, chopped
1/2 teaspoon onion powder
1/4 teaspoon Tabasco sauce
1/4 teaspoon freshly ground black pepper

1 cup chopped chives or green onion tops
2 lemons, cut into quarters

Makes 8 servings
Each serving contains approximately:
1-1/2 vegetable portions
38 calories
23 mg. sodium

Pour the entire contents of 1 can of tomatoes into a blender container. Pour only the juice from the second can of tomatoes into the blender. Dice the drained tomatoes from the second can and set aside. Add all remaining ingredients except chives and lemon quarters to the blender and blend until puréed. Pour the blended mixture into a large mixing bowl, add the diced tomatoes and mix well. Chill thoroughly. Garnish each serving with chives and a lemon wedge.

Serve Gazpacho with Toasted Tortilla Triangles as a first course before a Mexican-style luncheon or dinner party.

SHERRIED PEA SOUP

2 cups shelled peas (2 pounds unshelled)
1 cup Unsalted Chicken Stock, page 34
1/8 teaspoon white pepper
1 cup low-sodium low-fat milk
1/4 cup sherry
1/2 teaspoon freshly grated lemon peel

Makes 4 servings
Each serving contains approximately:
2 vegetable portions
1/4 low-fat milk portion
81 calories
4 mg. sodium

Combine the peas, chicken stock and white pepper in a saucepan with a lid. Bring to a boil, cover and cook until the peas are just tender, about 5 minutes. Cool slightly and put into a blender container. Add the milk and sherry and blend until smooth. Transfer the soup to a container, cover and chill. Serve in chilled bowls or in icers and sprinkle each serving with a pinch of grated lemon peel. This soup may also be served hot, though I personally prefer it cold.

BAKED FRENCH ONION SOUP

8 very thin slices French Bread
2 tablespoons unsalted butter or corn oil
    margarine
2 large onions, very thinly sliced, vertically
1/2 cup dry white wine
1/2 teaspoon freshly ground black pepper
Dash cayenne pepper
1 quart (4 cups) Unsalted Beef Stock,
    page 33, boiling
1 cup grated low-sodium Swiss-type cheese

Makes 4 servings
Each serving contains approximately:
1 vegetable portion
1-1/2 fat portions
1 starch portion
1 high-fat protein portion
258 calories
38 mg. sodium

Preheat the oven to 300°. Place the thin French Bread slices (2 slices together should be no more than the width of 1 normal slice) on a cookie sheet so they do not touch and place in the preheated 300° oven for about 5 minutes to dry. Set bread aside and turn the oven up to 325°.

Melt the butter or margarine in a large heavy iron skillet. Add the sliced onions, cover and cook over very low heat until onions are soft. Remove the lid and turn the heat up to high. Brown the onions, stirring constantly so that they do not burn. When they are nicely browned, turn the heat back down to low and add the wine. Continue cooking until the wine is almost completely absorbed. Add the black pepper and cayenne pepper and mix well. Add the beef stock, again mix well and simmer for 5 minutes. Divide the soup into 4 ovenproof bowls and place 2 slices dry French bread on top of each bowl. Allow to stand until the bread is completely

saturated with the soup, then sprinkle 1/4 cup of the grated cheese over each serving. Bake, uncovered, in the preheated 325° oven 30 to 40 minutes, or until the cheese is lightly browned. If you wish to hold the soup for a few minutes before serving, leave it in the oven, crack the door slightly and turn the oven off.

STRACCIATELLA ALLA ROMANA

1 quart (4 cups) Unsalted Chicken
   Stock, page 34
2 eggs
1/8 teaspoon ground nutmeg
1 tablespoon grated Romano cheese
2 tablespoons minced parsley

Makes 6 servings
Each serving contains approximately:
1/2 medium-fat protein portion
38 calories
46 mg. sodium

Bring the chicken stock to a boil in a saucepan. Combine the eggs, nutmeg and Romano cheese and beat thoroughly. Add the parsley to the beaten egg mixture and pour the entire mixture into the boiling stock, stirring continuously until the eggs are cooked. This only takes a minute. Immediately ladle the soup into 6 bowls and serve.

LENTIL SOUP

1 tablespoon unsalted butter or corn oil
  margarine
1 large onion, sliced
1 small green bell pepper, seeded and chopped
2 garlic buds, minced
2-1/2 quarts (10 cups) Unsalted Beef Stock,
  page 33
2 bay leaves
1 teaspoon dried thyme, crushed
1/4 teaspoon freshly ground black pepper
2 tablespoons Bakon Yeast

1 pound (2 cups) dried lentils, soaked in
  water to cover overnight and drained

Makes 8 servings
Each serving contains approximately:
1/4 vegetable portion
1-1/4 starch portions
1/4 fat portion
105 calories
42 mg. sodium

Heat the butter or margarine in a large iron skillet. Add the onion, green pepper and garlic and cook until the vegetables are tender and lightly brown. Put the beef stock in a large saucepan or soup kettle, add the cooked vegetables, bay leaves, thyme, pepper and Bakon Yeast and mix well. Then add the drained lentils and bring to a boil. Reduce heat, cover, leaving the lid ajar to allow the steam to escape, and simmer for 1-1/2 hours.

MINESTRONE

2 tablespoons olive oil
3 garlic buds, minced
1/2 pound lean pork, cut into 1/2-inch cubes
1 onion, finely chopped
2 medium zucchini, thinly sliced
1 leek, white part only, finely chopped
1/4 teaspoon freshly ground black pepper
1 teaspoon dried oregano, crushed
1 teaspoon dried basil, crushed
2-1/2 quarts (10 cups) Unsalted Beef Stock,
  page 33
1 cup dried kidney beans, soaked overnight
  in water to cover and drained
1 small head cabbage, shredded
6 large Romaine lettuce leaves, cut into strips

1/2 cup finely chopped parsley
1 cup dry red wine
1 16-ounce can unsalted tomatoes, with juice
1/2 cup elbow macaroni
2 tablespoons fresh lemon juice
1/3 cup freshly grated Parmesan cheese

Makes 16 servings
Each serving contains approximately:
1/4 medium-fat protein portion
1/4 fat portion
1/2 vegetable portion
1 starch portion
113 calories
41 mg. sodium

In a heavy iron skillet heat the olive oil, add the garlic and sauté until tender. Add the pork and sauté until browned and cooked. Add the onion, zucchini, leek, pepper, oregano and basil to the pork. Cover and cook for 10 minutes.

Bring the beef stock to a boil. Add the kidney beans and pork mixture and mix well. Then add the cabbage, lettuce, parsley and wine and cook until the beans are tender, about 1-1/2 hours. Add the tomatoes and their juice and the macaroni and cook 15 minutes longer. Just before serving, add the lemon juice and mix thoroughly. Sprinkle 1 scant teaspoon of the grated Parmesan cheese over the top of each serving.

SOPA DE ALBONDIGAS
(Mexican Meatball Soup)

Meatballs
1 pound ground lean round
1/2 cup minced onion
1 slice low-sodium bread, crumbled
1/4 cup low-sodium low-fat milk
1 egg, beaten
1/4 cup minced parsley
2 tablespoons minced fresh coriander
　　(cilantro)
1 teaspoon dried oregano, crushed
2 garlic buds, minced
1/2 teaspoon freshly ground black pepper
2 tablespoons chili powder

Soup
1 medium onion, diced
1 garlic bud, minced
1/2 teaspoon ground cumin
1 cup Unsalted Tomato Sauce, page 47
3 cups Unsalted Beef Stock, page 33
1 tablespoon fresh lemon juice
Dash Tabasco sauce (optional)

Makes 8 servings
Each serving contains approximately:
1-1/2 low-fat protein portions
1 vegetable portion
108 calories
85 mg. sodium

Combine all ingredients for the meatballs and mix well. Form the mixture into walnut-sized balls and set aside.

To make the soup, combine the onion, garlic, cumin, tomato sauce and stock in a large saucepan or soup kettle and bring to a boil. Reduce heat, add the meatballs and simmer, covered, for 40 minutes or until the meatballs are thoroughly cooked. Just before serving, add lemon juice and taste and adjust seasoning. If you wish a spicier soup, add a little Tabasco sauce.

This soup makes a wonderful luncheon entrée served with Toasted Tortilla Triangles and a tossed green salad.

sauces and gravies

"Sir Humphrey Davy
Detested gravy.
He lived in the odium
Of having discovered sodium."
—Edmund Clerihew Bentley (1875-1956)

When I wrote *The Calculating Cook,* I stated in the introduction to the sauce chapter that I felt like a sorcerer trying to make sauces taste like something that they really weren't. Now I realize I was only a sorcerer's apprentice, because omitting the salt and other high-sodium ingredients from sauces has taken a great deal more imagination and infinitely more hours of testing than anything I have ever done before. I am delighted with the results, however, and hope you will share my enthusiasm for the sauce recipes in this section. They are designed to help improve the overall flavor of a low-sodium diet.

DEFATTED DRIPPINGS

After cooking your roast beef, leg of lamb, chicken, turkey or whatever, remove it from the roasting pan and pour the drippings into a bowl. Put the bowl in the refrigerator until the drippings are cold and all of the fat has solidified on the top. Remove and discard the fat and you have defatted drippings.

Now, if you are in a hurry for the drippings because you want to serve them with your roast, put them in the freezer instead of the refrigerator and put the roast in a warm oven to keep it from cooling. After about 20 minutes you can remove the fat from the drippings, heat and serve them.

I always defat my drippings when I roast meat or poultry and keep them in the freezer. Defatted drippings add extra flavor to your stocks and are better than stocks for making gravies. In 1/2 cup, the calories are negligible and there are approximately 10 mg. sodium.

UNSALTED CHICKEN OR TURKEY GRAVY

2 cups defatted chicken or turkey drippings,
    page 45
2 cups Unsalted Chicken Stock or
    Unsalted Turkey Stock, page 34
3 tablespoons cornstarch or arrowroot
1/4 cup cold water
1 tablespoon unsalted butter or corn oil
    margarine
2 tablespoons minced onion
1 cup thinly sliced fresh mushrooms

Freshly ground black pepper to taste
Fresh lemon juice (optional)

Makes 2 to 3 cups
1/2 cup contains approximately:
3/4 fat portion
1/4 starch portion
52 calories
18 mg. sodium

Heat the defatted drippings and stock in a saucepan. Dissolve the cornstarch or arrowroot in the water and add to the saucepan. Cook slowly over medium heat, stirring occasionally, until the mixture thickens slightly. While the gravy is cooking, heat the butter or margarine in a skillet and add the minced onion. Cook until the onion is tender and then add the sliced mushrooms. Continue cooking until the mushrooms are tender and add to the gravy. Season to taste with pepper and a little fresh lemon juice, if desired.

UNSALTED BEEF GRAVY

1 cup defatted beef drippings, page 45
1 cup Unsalted Beef Stock, page 33
2 tablespoons cornstarch or arrowroot
1/4 cup cold water
1 tablespoon dried onion flakes
Freshly ground black pepper to taste
Dash Tabasco sauce (optional)

Makes about 1-1/2 cups
1/2 cup contains approximately:
1/2 starch portion
35 calories
11 mg. sodium

Heat the drippings and stock in a saucepan. Dissolve the cornstarch or arrowroot in the water and add to the saucepan. Cook slowly over medium heat, stirring occasionally, until thickened. Add onion flakes, pepper and Tabasco sauce, if desired.

UNSALTED TOMATO SAUCE (OR CATSUP)

1 quart unsalted tomato juice
1/4 cup red wine vinegar
3 garlic buds, cut in half
1 teaspoon fructose

Makes about 2-1/2 cups
1/4 cup contains approximately:
1/2 vegetable portion
13 calories
21 mg. sodium

Combine all ingredients in a saucepan and bring to a boil. Reduce heat to very low and simmer, uncovered, for 2 hours, stirring occasionally. Remove from heat and cool to room temperature. Remove the garlic buds and discard. Store the sauce in a nonmetal container in the refrigerator.

I suggest taking the time to make your own tomato sauce because commercial tomato sauce contains salt, and it is extremely difficult, if not impossible, to buy unsalted tomato sauce, a necessary ingredient for some of the recipes in this book.

UNSALTED COCKTAIL SAUCE

1 cup Unsalted Tomato Sauce, preceding
2 tablespoons fresh lemon juice
1 teaspoon grated fresh or unsalted prepared
   horseradish
Dash Tabasco sauce

Makes 1 cup
2 tablespoons contain approximately:
1/4 vegetable portion
7 calories
11 mg. sodium

Combine all ingredients and mix well. This cocktail sauce is good served over cold cooked fish and seafood, or as a low-calorie dip for raw vegetables.

MEXICAN COCKTAIL SAUCE

1 cup Unsalted Tomato Sauce, preceding
2 tablespoons fresh lemon juice
1/4 cup minced onion
1/2 cup finely chopped fresh coriander
   (cilantro)
Dash Tabasco sauce

Makes about 1-1/2 cups
2 tablespoons contain approximately:
1/4 vegetable portion
7 calories
11 mg. sodium

Combine all ingredients and mix well. This sauce is good with shellfish, cold fish, eggs and tacos.

MARINARA SAUCE

1/4 cup olive oil
1 medium onion, finely chopped
1 garlic bud, minced
5 cups Unsalted Tomato Sauce, page 47
1-1/2 cups unsalted tomato paste (2 6-ounce cans)
1 quart water
1/4 teaspoon freshly ground black pepper
1 teaspoon dried oregano, crushed

1 teaspoon dried basil, crushed

Makes about 1-1/2 quarts (6 cups)
1/2 cup contains approximately:
1 fat portion
2 vegetable portions
95 calories
49 mg. sodium

Heat the olive oil in a large saucepan. Add the onion and garlic and sauté until soft and a golden brown in color. Add all remaining ingredients and mix thoroughly. Bring to a boil, reduce heat and simmer, uncovered, for at least 2 hours. Store in a nonmetal container in the refrigerator.

MUSTARD SAUCE

4 teaspoons dry mustard
1/4 cup cider vinegar
2 eggs, lightly beaten
1/2 cup low-sodium low-fat milk
1 tablespoon unsalted butter or corn oil
   margarine
3 tablespoons fructose

Makes about 1-1/2 cups
2 tablespoons contain approximately:
1/4 fat portion
1/4 fruit portion
1/4 medium-fat protein portion
40 calories
10 mg. sodium

Combine the dry mustard with the vinegar and stir until the mustard is completely dissolved. Combine the mustard-vinegar mixture with the eggs and milk in a saucepan. Bring slowly to a boil, stirring constantly with a wire whisk. When the boil is reached, continue stirring for 30 seconds. Remove from the heat and set the butter or margarine on top of the sauce. *Do not stir.* Allow to cool to room temperature. Add the fructose, and with a wire whisk, mix the sauce thoroughly. Store in the refrigerator.

UNSALTED WHITE SAUCE

2 cups low-sodium low-fat milk
1 tablespoon unsalted butter or corn oil
   margarine
3 tablespoons all-purpose flour
1/8 teaspoon white pepper

Makes 1-1/2 cups

1/2 cup contains approximately:
1-1/2 fat portions
1/2 starch portion
1 low-fat milk portion
228 calories
7 mg. sodium

Put the milk in a saucepan on low heat and bring just to the boiling point. In another saucepan, melt the butter or margarine, add the flour and cook, stirring constantly, for 3 minutes. *Do not brown.* Remove from the heat and add the simmering milk all at once, stirring constantly with a wire whisk. Put the sauce back on the heat and cook slowly for 30 minutes, stirring occasionally. (If you wish a thicker sauce, cook it a little longer.) Add the pepper and stir in well.

Note If there are lumps in the sauce (though there shouldn't be by this method), whirl it in the blender.

UNSALTED LIGHT BROWN SAUCE

1 quart (4 cups) Unsalted Beef Stock, page 33
2 tablespoons finely chopped shallots
1/2 cup Burgundy
1/4 cup sherry
1/4 cup dry white wine
4 tablespoons cornstarch
1/4 cup cold water
1/2 teaspoon freshly ground black pepper

Dash Tabasco sauce

Makes about 4 cups (1 quart)
1/2 cup contains approximately:
1/4 starch portion
17 calories
7 mg. sodium

In a saucepan, heat the stock. In another pan, combine the shallots and wines and place over fairly high heat, boiling the mixture until reduced by one-third. When reduced, add the heated stock and then lower the heat to medium. Allow the mixture to come to a simmering boil. Dissolve the cornstarch in the cold water and add it to the simmering sauce, mixing thoroughly with a wire whisk. Add pepper and Tabasco sauce, taste and adjust seasonings.

This is called "light" brown sauce because it lacks the rich, dark brown color associated with classic French brown sauce. The distinctive color is obtained either by adding caramel coloring, which though perfectly acceptable in a low-sodium diet is difficult to find, or Kitchen Bouquet, which is high in sodium. Therefore, unless you can find the caramel coloring, you will have to opt for a lighter version of the classic.

HOLLANDAISE SAUCE SANS SEL

3 egg yolks
2 tablespoons fresh lemon juice
Pinch cayenne pepper
6 tablespoons unsalted butter or corn oil
    margarine, melted
3 egg whites
1/8 teaspoon cream of tartar

Makes 1-1/2 cups
2 tablespoons contain approximately:
1/4 medium-fat protein portion
1-1/2 fat portions
87 calories
15 mg. sodium

Place the egg yolks, lemon juice and cayenne pepper in a blender container. Cover the blender and blend at high speed 2 to 3 seconds. Reduce the speed to medium. Remove the lid but leave the blender running and slowly pour in the butter or margarine in a very thin stream. (If you are not going to use the sauce immediately, set the blender container into a pan of lukewarm water so that the sauce will not separate.) Combine the egg whites and cream of tartar and beat until stiff but not dry. Fold the egg whites into the sauce until it is a smooth but still a very light mixture.

Adding the egg whites to the sauce lightens it and doubles the amount, so that there are fewer calories per serving.

BÉARNAISE SAUCE SANS SEL

1/4 cup red wine vinegar
1/4 cup dry white wine
1 tablespoon minced shallots or green onion
    tops
2 teaspoons dried tarragon, crushed
1/8 teaspoon freshly ground black pepper
Pinch cayenne pepper
3 egg yolks
6 tablespoons unsalted butter or corn oil
    margarine, melted

3 egg whites
1/8 teaspoon cream of tartar
2 tablespoons minced fresh parsley

Makes 1-1/2 cups
2 tablespoons contain approximately:
1/4 medium-fat protein portion
1-1/2 fat portions
87 calories
19 mg. sodium

Combine the vinegar, wine, shallots, tarragon and black and cayenne peppers in a saucepan and boil until reduced to 2 tablespoons. Allow to cool to room temperature. Combine the egg yolks and cooled vinegar mixture in a blender container. Blend at high speed for 2 seconds. Reduce speed to medium. Remove the lid but leave the blender running and slowly pour in the butter or margarine in a very thin stream. (If you are not going to use the sauce immediately, set the blender container in a pan of lukewarm water so that the sauce will not separate.) Combine the egg whites and cream of tartar and beat until stiff but not dry. Fold the egg whites and parsley into the egg yolk mixture until it is a smooth but still a very light mixture.

The egg whites do the same thing for béarnaise that they do for the hollandaise—lighten and double the amount, therefore reducing the number of calories per serving.

UNSALTED MAYONNAISE

1 egg
1 teaspoon dry mustard
Pinch of cayenne pepper
1 tablespoon fresh lemon juice
1-1/2 teaspoons red wine vinegar
1 cup corn oil

Makes 1-1/2 cups
1 tablespoon contains approximately:
2 fat portions
90 calories
3 mg. sodium

Dip the whole egg (in the shell) in boiling water for 30 seconds. Remove the egg from the water and break into a blender container. Add the mustard and cayenne pepper and blend for approximately 30 seconds or until the mixture is thick and foamy. Add the lemon juice and vinegar and blend for a few more seconds. Uncover the blender, and running it at medium speed, slowly add the corn oil in a very thin stream into the exact center of the container. Blend only until the proper consistency is reached.

It is extremely important to add the oil very slowly or the mayonnaise will separate. If it does separate, warm a mixing bowl, place a very small amount of the separated mayonnaise in it and beat with a wire whisk for several seconds until it starts to thicken. Add the rest of the mayonnaise, 1 teaspoon at a time, continuing to beat with the whisk. This is a slow process, but it is the only way I know to recombine separated mayonnaise.

This mayonnaise is so much better than any mayonnaise I have ever tasted that I do not think you will ever want to go back to using a commercial product.

SECRET TARTAR SAUCE

2/3 cup sour cream
2 tablespoons Unsalted Mayonnaise,
   preceding
1-1/2 teaspoons fresh lemon juice
1/4 teaspoon fructose
2 tablespoons Dilled Onion Relish, page 81

Makes 1 cup
1 tablespoon contains approximately:
1/4 vegetable portion
1/2 fat portion
30 calories
5 mg. sodium

In a mixing bowl, combine the sour cream, mayonnaise, lemon juice and fructose and mix well. Add the Dilled Onion Relish and again mix well.

This tartar sauce is not only lower in sodium than most other tartar sauces, but it is also lower in calories. I have named it Secret Tartar Sauce because the real surprise comes when you find it also tastes better than most other tartar sauces.

DILL SAUCE

1/2 cup Unsalted Mayonnaise, preceding
1 cup low-fat plain yogurt
1 teaspoon dried tarragon, crushed
1-1/2 teaspoons dried dill weed, crushed
1 teaspoon fresh lemon juice

Makes about 1-1/2 cups
2 tablespoons contain approximately:
1-1/2 fat portions
68 calories
12 mg. sodium

Put the mayonnaise and yogurt in a mixing bowl and mix thoroughly with a wire whisk. Add the herbs and lemon juice and again mix thoroughly. Pour into a container with a tight-fitting lid and refrigerate.

This sauce is even better 2 days after it is made. It is delicious on vegetables and seafood, especially Salmon Quenelles.

ORIENTAL SESAME SEED SAUCE

1/4 cup sesame seeds
2/3 cup corn oil
2 tablespoons fresh lemon juice
2 tablespoons sherry
2 tablespoons fructose
1 teaspoon garlic powder

Makes about 1 cup
1 tablespoon contains approximately:
2-1/2 fat portions
113 calories
2 mg. sodium

Preheat the oven to 350°. Place the sesame seeds on a cookie sheet in the center of the preheated 350° oven for about 8 to 10 minutes, or until a golden brown. Watch them carefully as they burn easily. Set aside.

Combine all remaining ingredients and mix well. Add the toasted sesame seeds to the mixture and put in a jar with a tight-fitting lid. Shake vigorously for 1 full minute. Place in the refrigerator for at least 24 hours before using.

This is a versatile sauce. It is one of my favorite salad dressings, is excellent as a marinade for both fish and chicken, and is also a good sauce for fruit, vegetables, fish, meat and poultry. I sometimes thicken it with a little pectin and use it as a dip for raw or cold cooked vegetables.

LEMON BARBECUE SAUCE

1/2 cup fresh lemon juice
1/2 teaspoon freshly ground black pepper
1 teaspoon liquid smoke
1 teaspoon dried thyme, crushed
2 tablespoons grated onion
2 buds garlic, minced
1/4 cup corn oil

Makes 3/4 cup
2 tablespoons contain approximately:
2 fat portions
90 calories
1 mg. sodium

Combine the lemon juice, pepper, liquid smoke and thyme in a small mixing bowl and mix well. Add all other ingredients and again mix well. Cover and refrigerate for at least 24 hours before using. This is an excellent barbecue sauce for fish and poultry.

MAJOR JONES CHUTNEY

3/4 pound tart green apples, unpeeled and
   finely chopped (2 apples or about 2 cups)
1 cup finely chopped raisins
1 teaspoon corn oil
1 teaspoon ground mustard seed or crushed
   whole mustard seeds
1 teaspoon ground coriander
3/4 teaspoon ground ginger
3/4 teaspoon chili powder
1/4 teaspoon ground turmeric
1/4 teaspoon ground cumin

1/4 teaspoon garlic powder
1/8 teaspoon cayenne pepper
2-1/2 tablespoons red wine vinegar
1-1/2 cups water

Makes 2 cups
2 tablespoons contain approximately:
3/4 fruit portion
30 calories
5 mg. sodium

Combine the chopped apples and raisins in a large mixing bowl. Mix thoroughly and set aside. Heat the oil in a heavy saucepan and add all of the spices, mixing well. Combine the vinegar and the water, add to the spice mixture and bring to a boil. Then add the apple-raisin mixture and cook, uncovered, over low heat, stirring occasionally, for about 1 hour and 15 minutes, or until the liquid is absorbed and the apples are completely tender. Cool to room temperature and store in a covered container in the refrigerator.

The importance of making your own chutney is that commercial chutney is so high in sodium. In Major Grey's Chutney, made by Crosse & Blackwell, there are 588 milligrams of sodium in 2 tablespoons compared to only 5 milligrams of sodium for Major Jones Chutney.

HONEY BUTTER

1/4 cup unsalted butter or corn oil
   margarine, at room temperature
1 cup spun honey, at room temperature

Makes 1-1/4 cups

1 tablespoon contains approximately:
1/2 fat portion
1 fruit portion
63 calories
1 mg. sodium

Combine the butter or margarine with the honey and mix thoroughly. This is a delicious spread for toast, pancakes, waffles and French toast. It is also delicious on fresh fruit or ice cream.

LOW-SODIUM JELLED MILK

1 envelope (1 scant tablespoon) unflavored
   gelatin
2 tablespoons cold water
1/4 cup boiling water
1 cup low-sodium low-fat milk

Makes 1 cup
1 cup contains approximately:
1 low-fat milk portion
125 calories
12.5 mg. sodium

Soften the gelatin in 2 tablespoons cold water. Add the boiling water and stir until the gelatin is completely dissolved. Add the milk and mix well. Place the gelatin-milk mixture in a covered container in the refrigerator. When it is jelled, it is ready to use.

   Mix jelled milk with an equal amount of cold low-sodium low-fat milk in the blender and use it over fruit or cereal. The thick, creamy consistency makes the milk seem richer.

EGG-AND-MILK CEREAL TOPPING

1 egg
1 cup low-sodium low-fat milk
3/4 teaspoon fructose
1/4 teaspoon vanilla extract

Makes 1 serving

Each serving contains approximately:
1 medium-fat protein portion
1 low-fat milk portion
1/4 fruit portion
210 calories
72 mg. sodium

Dip the whole egg (in the shell) in boiling water for 30 seconds. Remove the egg from the boiling water and break it into a blender container. Add all remaining ingredients and blend until frothy. Pour this topping over cereal for a high-protein, low-sodium breakfast treat. Top it with some fresh fruit and you have your entire meal in one bowl.

salad dressings

You can't create a great salad without first creating a great salad dressing. Like sauces, good-tasting low-sodium salad dressings are difficult, though not impossible, to achieve. In the Secret Salad Dressing series, I have tried to include a wide variety of herbs and spices in the hope of providing something for everyone.

Many of the salad dressings in this section also make excellent marinades for cold cooked vegetables, fish, meat and poultry. Marinate poultry and red meats for at least 24 hours before cooking.

SECRET BASIC DRESSING

1/4 cup red wine vinegar
1/4 teaspoon garlic powder
1/4 teaspoon dry mustard
1/2 teaspoon fructose
1/4 cup water
1/4 teaspoon freshly ground black pepper
2 tablespoons fresh lemon juice

1 cup corn oil

Makes 1-1/2 cups
1 tablespoon contains approximately:
2 fat portions
90 calories
Trace mg. sodium

Combine the vinegar, garlic powder, dry mustard and fructose and stir until the dry ingredients are thoroughly dissolved. Add the water, pepper and lemon juice and mix well. Slowly stir in the oil. Pour into a jar with a tight-fitting lid and shake vigorously for 2 full minutes. Store, covered, in the refrigerator.

SECRET CURRY DRESSING

1/2 teaspoon curry powder
1/8 teaspoon ground ginger
1-1/2 cups Secret Basic Dressing, preceding

Makes 1-1/2 cups

1 tablespoon contains approximately:
2 fat portions
90 calories
Trace mg. sodium

Add the curry powder and ginger to the Secret Basic Dressing and mix thoroughly.

This amount of curry creates a rather subtle flavor, particularly in the absence of salt. If you want a stronger curry flavor, increase the curry powder to 1 teaspoon.

SECRET CAESAR DRESSING

1/2 teaspoon fructose
1/4 cup red wine vinegar
1/4 cup water
1/4 teaspoon freshly ground black pepper
1/4 teaspoon dry mustard
1/4 cup fresh lemon juice
1 garlic bud, minced
1/4 cup freshly grated Parmesan cheese

1 cup Garlic Oil, following (see Note)

Makes 1-1/2 cups
1 tablespoon contains approximately:
2-1/2 fat portions
113 calories
9 mg. sodium

Dissolve the fructose in the vinegar. Add all remaining ingredients, except the Garlic Oil, and mix well. Slowly stir in the oil. Place in a jar with a tight-fitting lid and shake vigorously for 1 full minute. Store, covered, in the refrigerator.

This dressing is so good that many Caesar salad buffs have no idea that they are eating a low-sodium version.

Note If you do not have Garlic Oil already prepared, 24 hours before making this dressing add 4 garlic buds to 1 cup of corn oil in a jar with a tight-fitting lid and allow to stand at room temperature. Remove the garlic from the oil and proceed as directed in the recipe.

GARLIC OIL

4 cups corn oil
14 large garlic buds, cut in half

Makes 4 cups

1 tablespoon contains approximately:
3 fat portions
135 calories
Trace mg. sodium

Add the garlic to the corn oil in a jar with a tight-fitting lid and allow to stand at room temperature for 1 month. Strain out garlic and use the oil for cooking or as a dressing for salads, cooked vegetables or plain pasta.

SECRET VINAIGRETTE DRESSING

2 tablespoons chopped pimiento
2 tablespoons finely chopped chives
2 tablespoons finely chopped parsley
1 hard-cooked egg, finely chopped
1/8 teaspoon paprika
Dash Tabasco sauce
1-1/2 cups Secret Basic Dressing, page 57

Makes 2 cups
1 tablespoon contains approximately:
1-3/4 fat portions
79 calories
2 mg. sodium

Add all ingredients to the Secret Basic Dressing and mix thoroughly. Store, covered, in the refrigerator.

I approach vinaigrette dressing much the way the French cook approaches a cassoulet—use what is available. I chop up any raw or cold cooked vegetable that is low in sodium and add it. For a spicier vinaigrette, add a little Dilled Onion Relish.

SECRET TARRAGON DRESSING

1 tablespoon dried tarragon, crushed
1-1/2 cups Secret Basic Dressing, page 57

Makes 1-1/2 cups

1 tablespoon contains approximately:
2 fat portions
90 calories
Trace mg. sodium

Add the crushed tarragon to the Secret Basic Dressing and mix thoroughly. Store, covered, in the refrigerator.

SECRET CUMIN DRESSING

1/2 teaspoon ground cumin
1/8 teaspoon chili powder
1-1/2 cups Secret Basic Dressing, page 57

Makes 1-1/2 cups

1 tablespoon contains approximately:
2 fat portions
90 calories
Trace mg. sodium

Add the cumin and chili powder to the Secret Basic Dressing and mix thoroughly. Store, covered, in the refrigerator.

This dressing improves in flavor if allowed to stand for 24 hours before using. If you prefer a stronger cumin flavor, add more cumin to taste.

SECRET ITALIAN DRESSING

2 teaspoons dried oregano
1 teaspoon dried basil
1 teaspoon dried tarragon
1/2 teaspoon fructose
1-1/2 cups Secret Basic Dressing, page 57

Makes 1-1/2 cups
1 tablespoon contains approximately:
2 fat portions
90 calories
Trace mg. sodium

Combine the oregano, basil and tarragon, and using a mortar and pestle, crush them together thoroughly. Add the crushed herb mixture and the fructose to the Secret Basic Dressing and mix thoroughly. Store, covered, in the refrigerator.

This dressing is also good for marinating cold cooked vegetables for antipasto, the first course of an Italian meal, or as a marinade for fish, poultry and meat.

SECRET FENNEL DRESSING

1 teaspoon fennel seeds, crushed
1-1/2 cups Secret Basic Dressing, page 57

Makes 1-1/2 cups

1 tablespoon contains approximately:
2 fat portions
90 calories
Trace mg. sodium

Add the fennel seeds to the Secret Basic Dressing and mix thoroughly. Store, covered, in the refrigerator.

FIESTA DRESSING

2 cups unsalted canned tomatoes
1/4 cup fresh lemon juice
2 tablespoons red wine vinegar
3 tablespoons finely chopped onion
2 garlic buds, chopped
1/4 teaspoon chili powder
1/4 teaspoon dried oregano, crushed
1/4 teaspoon ground cumin

1/4 teaspoon freshly ground black pepper
1/8 teaspoon Tabasco sauce

Makes 2 cups
2 tablespoons contains approximately:
1/4 vegetable portion
7 calories
9 mg. sodium

Put all ingredients into a blender container and blend until smooth. Store, covered, in the refrigerator. This low-sodium, low-calorie, low-cholesterol dressing is perfect for the dieter, plus it tastes fantastic.

VI'S CELERY SEED DRESSING

2 tablespoons fructose
1/4 cup tarragon wine vinegar
2 tablespoons fresh lemon juice
1/4 teaspoon freshly ground black pepper
1/2 teaspoon onion powder
1/4 cup water
1-1/2 teaspoons celery seeds, crushed

1 cup corn oil

Makes 1-1/2 cups
1 tablespoon contains approximately:
2 fat portions
90 calories
1 mg. sodium

Dissolve the fructose in the vinegar. Combine all ingredients, except the corn oil, and mix thoroughly. Slowly stir in the corn oil. Pour into a jar with a tight-fitting lid and shake vigorously for a full minute. Store, covered, in the refrigerator.

ORANGE-ONION DRESSING

1/4 cup white wine vinegar
1/2 teaspoon fructose
1/4 teaspoon dry mustard
1/4 cup fresh orange juice
1/4 teaspoon freshly ground black pepper
1/2 medium onion, chopped
1 cup corn oil

Makes 1-1/2 cups
1 tablespoon contains approximately:
2 fat portions
90 calories
1 mg. sodium

Combine all ingredients, except the corn oil, in a blender container and blend until the onion is liquified. Pour the mixture into a jar with a tight-fitting lid and add the corn oil. Cover and shake the mixture vigorously for 30 seconds. Store, covered, in the refrigerator.

BANANA CREAM DRESSING

2 small ripe bananas, sliced
1 teaspoon fresh lemon juice
2 cups (1 pint) low-fat plain yogurt
1 teaspoon coconut extract
1/2 teaspoon vanilla extract

Makes 2-1/2 cups
1/2 cup contains approximately:
3/4 fruit portion
1/2 low-fat milk portion
93 calories
46 mg. sodium

Combine the sliced bananas and lemon juice in a blender container and blend until smooth. Add all remaining ingredients and blend again until smooth. Store, covered, in the refrigerator.

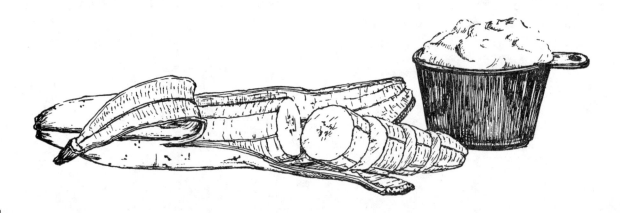

CURRIED GINGER DRESSING

1 cup (1/2 pint) sour cream
1/4 cup Unsalted Mayonnaise, page 52
3/4 teaspoon curry powder
1/4 teaspoon ground ginger
2 teaspoons fresh lemon juice

Makes 1-1/2 cups

1/4 cup contains approximately:
2-1/2 fat portions
113 calories
17 mg. sodium

1 tablespoon contains approximately:
3/4 fat portion
34 calories
4 mg. sodium

Combine all ingredients in a blender container and blend until smooth. Store, covered, in the refrigerator.

Curried Coconut Dressing Variation Add 1/2 teaspoon coconut extract to the Curried Ginger Dressing and proceed as directed.

CURRIED APPLESAUCE DRESSING

3/4 cup unsweetened applesauce
2 tablespoons fresh lemon juice
1 tablespoon white wine vinegar
1/2 teaspoon vanilla extract
1/2 teaspoon ground cinnamon
1/4 teaspoon curry powder
1/8 teaspoon ground ginger

1/2 cup corn oil

Makes 1-1/2 cups
1 tablespoon contains approximately:
1 fat portion
45 calories
Trace mg. sodium

Combine all ingredients, except the corn oil, and mix thoroughly. Add the corn oil and again mix well. Store, covered, in the refrigerator.

salads

Salads have great latitude in a menu. They can be either light and low calorie and served before, with or after the entrée, or they can include all of the nutrition necessary for a balanced meal and be served as the main course.

Get in the habit of taking a few extra minutes to decorate your salads and always serve them on chilled plates. When using lettuce or other greens, wash them thoroughly a couple of hours before you plan to serve the salad. Pat the greens dry with paper towels, tear them into bite-size pieces and place in a colander. Put the colander on top of a plate to drain and put in the refrigerator until serving time. You will find that your salads will be crisper and require less salad dressing, because the dressing will not be diluted by unwanted water.

ITALIAN EGGPLANT ANTIPASTO

1 medium eggplant
1/4 cup fresh lemon juice
White pepper
1 cup Secret Italian Dressing, page 60
1 large ripe tomato, peeled and diced
1 large onion, diced
1/2 cup finely chopped parsley

Makes 6 servings
Each serving contains approximately:
1-1/2 fat portions
1 vegetable portion
93 calories
9 mg. sodium

Peel the eggplant and slice it in 1/4-inch-thick slices. Spread the eggplant slices in a glass baking dish and pour the lemon juice over them. Sprinkle both sides of the slices lightly with white pepper, cover the dish and allow to stand for at least 1 hour. Pour off the liquid. Then steam the eggplant over rapidly boiling water until just fork tender, about 5 minutes. Be careful not to overcook the eggplant or it will be mushy.

Put the eggplant back in the glass baking dish, pour the dressing over it and allow to cool to room temperature. Sprinkle the tomato and onion evenly over the top of the eggplant, cover the dish and refrigerate for at least 3 hours before serving. Serve on chilled plates and sprinkle with parsley.

CURRIED ORANGE APPETIZER

6 large oranges, peeled and thinly sliced
1 cup Secret Curry Dressing, page 57
1 large onion, diced
Parsley sprigs for garnish

Makes 8 servings

Each serving contains approximately:
1 fruit portion
1 fat portion
85 calories
2 mg. sodium

Spread the orange slices in a glass baking dish and pour the dressing over them. Sprinkle the onion evenly over the orange slices, cover and refrigerate for at least 3 hours before serving. Serve on chilled plates garnished with parsley sprigs.

This is an ideal appetizer, salad or cold course for a buffet because it is easy to serve and attractive.

VEGETARIAN CHEF'S SALAD

1/4 cup sunflower seeds
1/2 large head iceberg lettuce, shredded
   (about 4 cups)
2 medium tomatoes, diced
1 cup chopped raw broccoli
1/2 cup alfalfa sprouts
1/2 cup bean sprouts
1 cup diced low-sodium cheddar cheese
1/2 cup Secret Tarragon Dressing, page 59

Makes 4 servings
Each serving contains approximately:
1 vegetable portion
5 fat portions
1 high-fat protein portion
345 calories
32 mg. sodium

Preheat the oven to 350°. Put the sunflower seeds on a cookie sheet in the preheated 350° oven for approximately 10 minutes, or until a golden brown. Watch them carefully as they burn easily. Set aside.

Combine all remaining ingredients and toss thoroughly. Divide onto 4 chilled plates. Sprinkle 1 tablespoon of the toasted sunflower seeds on each salad.

CURRY CONDIMENT SALAD

1/4 cup unsweetened shredded coconut
1 large head iceberg lettuce, torn into bite-
    size pieces (about 8 cups)
2 tablespoons finely chopped unsalted dry-
    roasted peanuts
1/4 cup raisins
4 hard-cooked eggs, chopped
2 red apples, cored and diced
1/2 cup Curried Ginger Dressing, page 63

Mint or parsley sprigs for garnish

Makes 6 servings
Each serving contains approximately:
3/4 medium-fat protein portion
3/4 fruit portion
1-1/2 fat portions
154 calories
53 mg. sodium

Preheat the oven to 350°. Place the shredded coconut on a cookie sheet in the preheated 350° oven for approximately 8 minutes, or until golden brown. Watch it carefully as it burns easily. Set aside.

    Combine all remaining ingredients and toss thoroughly. Divide evenly onto chilled plates and garnish with mint or parsley sprigs. Sprinkle each serving with 2 teaspoons toasted coconut.

    I like to serve this salad as the main course for luncheons with Banana Nut Bread and as a side dish for fish and poultry entrées at dinner.

APPLE AND CHEESE SALAD

1/2 cup chopped walnuts
1 large head iceberg lettuce, chopped (about
    8 cups)
3 medium Delicious apples, diced (about
    4 cups)
2 cups diced unsalted farmer's cheese (1/2 pound)
3/4 cup Secret Italian Dressing, page 60

Makes 6 servings
Each serving contains approximately:
1/2 fruit portion
1-1/4 low-fat protein portions
4 fat portions
268 calories
19 mg. sodium

Preheat the oven to 350°. Place the walnuts on a cookie sheet in the preheated 350° oven for approximately 10 minutes, or until a golden brown. Watch them carefully as they burn easily. Set aside. Combine all remaining ingredients and toss well. Divide evenly onto chilled plates. Sprinkle a rounded tablespoon of the toasted walnuts evenly over each serving.

    This is my favorite salad in this book. It is similar to Jeanne Appleseed Salad in *Fabulous Fiber Cookbook,* but in this recipe I have used walnuts instead of sunflower seeds. The walnuts add more flavor, thus better offsetting the greatly reduced amount of sodium.

PINEAPPLE AND CHEESE SALAD

1/2 cup chopped walnuts
1 large head iceberg lettuce, finely chopped
   (about 8 cups)
1 20-ounce can crushed pineapple in natural
   juice, drained
3 cups diced unsalted farmer's cheese
   (3/4 pound)
3/4 cup Orange-Onion Dressing, page 62

Makes 6 servings
Each serving contains approximately:
1 fruit portion
4 fat portions
2 low-fat protein portions
330 calories
26 mg. sodium

Preheat the oven to 350°. Place the walnuts on a cookie sheet in the preheated 350° oven for approximately 10 minutes, or until golden brown. Watch them carefully as they burn easily. Set aside. Combine all remaining ingredients and toss well. Divide evenly onto chilled plates. Sprinkle a rounded tablespoon of the toasted walnuts evenly over each serving.

    This salad is a good accompaniment to roasted poultry or pork, or serve as a light luncheon salad with Banana Nut Bread.

EAST INDIAN TUNA SALAD

6 small heads Boston lettuce
1 20-ounce can crushed pineapple in natural
   juice, undrained
3 6-1/2-ounce cans low-sodium tuna, drained
1/2 cup raisins, finely chopped
3/4 cup Curried Coconut Dressing, page 63

Makes 6 servings
Each serving contains approximately:
1-1/2 low-fat protein portions
1-1/2 fruit portions
1-1/2 fat portions
211 calories
60 mg. sodium

Remove the hearts from the heads of lettuce, being careful not to separate or tear the outer leaves. Wash the hearts, tear them into bite-size pieces (approximately 8 cups torn lettuce) and put into a large bowl. Retain the outer leaves for lettuce "bowls" in which to serve the salad. Wash them carefully and place on paper towels in the refrigerator until needed. Add the pineapple and its juice to the torn lettuce. Drain the tuna, separate it into bite-size pieces and add it to the lettuce and pineapple. Add the raisins and dressing and toss well. Place each lettuce bowl on a large chilled plate. Evenly divide the salad into the 6 lettuce bowls.

    I like to serve this salad for luncheons with Giant Cinnamon Popovers and Cold Orange Soufflé for dessert.

CHINESE PEA POD AND SHRIMP SALAD

1 small head cauliflower, separated into bite-
   size flowerets (about 3 cups)
1/2 pound pea pods (snow peas)
1 pound shelled cooked shrimp (about 3 cups)
1/2 cup Oriental Sesame Seed Sauce, page 53

Each serving contains approximately:
1-1/2 vegetable portions
1-1/2 low-fat protein portions
2 fat portions
211 calories
70 mg. sodium

Makes 6 servings

Steam the cauliflower over rapidly boiling water for 3 minutes. Add the pea pods and cook for 2 more minutes. Remove from the heat and immediately place under cold running water. Drain thoroughly and place in a large mixing bowl. Cover and refrigerate until thoroughly chilled. Add the shrimp and Oriental Sesame Seed Sauce and toss thoroughly. Serve for lunch with chopsticks.

Variation For a lower sodium salad, substitute an equal amount of cooked chicken breast meat cut into julienne (strips 1/4 inch wide by 2 inches in length) for the shrimp. When using chicken, the milligrams of sodium per serving are only 48.

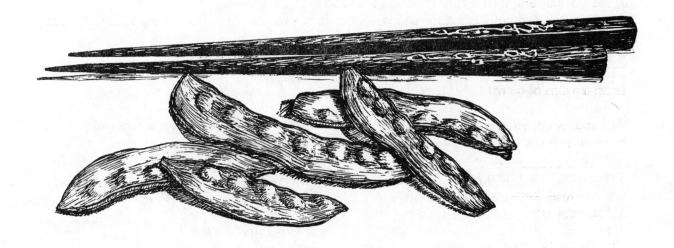

RAINBOW CHICKEN SALAD

4 heads Boston lettuce
2 cups diced cooked chicken
2 medium oranges, peeled and chopped
(1 cup)
1 cup chopped fresh pineapple or canned
pineapple chunks in natural juice,
drained
1 cup Banana Cream Dressing, page 62
1 cup fresh or unsweetened frozen blueberries,
thawed

Ground cinnamon for garnish

Makes 4 servings
Each serving contains approximately:
1-1/2 fruit portions
2 low-fat protein portions
1/4 low-fat milk portion
202 calories
77 mg. sodium

Remove the hearts from the heads of lettuce, being careful not to separate or tear the outer leaves. Wash the hearts, tear them into bite-size pieces (approximately 5 cups torn lettuce) and put into a large bowl. Retain the outer leaves for lettuce "bowls" in which to serve the salad. Wash them carefully and place on paper towels in the refrigerator until needed. Add the chicken, oranges, pineapple and dressing to the torn lettuce and toss well. Place each lettuce "bowl" on a chilled salad plate and evenly divide the salad into them. Spoon 1/4 cup of the blueberries on top of each serving and then lightly sprinkle each salad with cinnamon.

This salad is both beautiful and delicious. It is a lovely entrée for a light lunch or supper menu. Serve it with Gingerbread Muffins.

ST. PATRICK'S DAY POTATO SALAD
(with a touch of green)

2 pounds white potatoes (8 to 10 small)
1 pound young string beans
1/4 cup dry vermouth
1 teaspoon fresh lemon juice
1/4 teaspoon freshly ground black pepper
1/4 cup olive oil
1/4 cup corn oil
1/4 cup finely sliced green onions, including
the tops
2 tablespoons finely minced fresh dill, or
1 tablespoon dried dill weed, crushed

2 tablespoons finely chopped parsley
Parsley sprigs for garnish

Makes 8 servings
Each serving contains approximately:
1 starch portion
3/4 vegetable portion
3 fat portions
224 calories
12 mg. sodium

Put the potatoes into a large pot with water to cover, bring to a boil and boil until just tender; do not overcook. Drain the potatoes and allow them to cool until they can be easily handled.

While the potatoes are cooling, remove the ends and strings from the beans and cut each bean on the diagonal (French style) into 3 or 4 pieces. Steam the beans over rapidly boiling water for 5 to 7 minutes, or until crisp tender. Remove from the heat and immediately place under cold running water until thoroughly cool. Drain the beans on a towel and set aside.

Peel the cooled cooked potatoes and cut them lengthwise into 1/4-inch-thick strips. Put the strips into a large mixing bowl and set aside. Put the vermouth, lemon juice and pepper in a jar with a tight-fitting lid and shake until well mixed. Add the oils and shake vigorously for a full minute. Add the green onions, dill and parsley and shake well again. Pour the dressing over the potatoes and mix well. Cover the bowl and allow to stand for 1 hour. Then add the green beans and toss well. Garnish with parsley sprigs.

This is one of the few salads I prefer served at room temperature rather than chilled. It is a good first course served on lettuce leaves or a good vegetable side dish served with boiled beef for a St. Patrick's Day party.

P.M. SALAD
(peanuts and mushrooms)

2 cups thinly sliced fresh mushrooms
   (1/2 pound)
2 tablespoons fresh lemon juice
3/4 cup low-sodium low-fat milk
1/2 teaspoon fructose
3/4 teaspoon curry powder
1/4 teaspoon onion powder
Dash white pepper
1 tablespoon corn oil
1 head Boston lettuce, torn in bite-size
   pieces (4 to 5 cups)

1/4 cup chopped unsalted dry-roasted
   peanuts

Makes 6 servings
Each serving contains approximately:
1 vegetable portion
1 fat portion
70 calories
11 mg. sodium

Combine the mushrooms and lemon juice in a nonmetal bowl. Cover and refrigerate until ready to use. Combine the milk, fructose, curry powder, onion powder and white pepper in a bowl and mix thoroughly, using a wire whisk, until a creamy consistency. Beat in the oil. Cover and refrigerate until ready to use. Just before serving, toss together the Boston lettuce, sliced mushrooms and dressing and divide evenly onto 6 chilled salad plates. Sprinkle chopped peanuts evenly over each serving.

MYSTERY SLAW

1 20-ounce can crushed pineapple in natural
  juice, undrained
1 teaspoon fructose
1-1/2 teaspoons coconut extract
1 head raw cauliflower, finely grated
  (about 4 cups)
Ground cinnamon for garnish

Mint sprigs for garnish (optional)

Makes 6 servings
Each serving contains approximately:
1 fruit portion
40 calories
9 mg. sodium

Pour the juice off the pineapple into a large bowl and set the crushed pineapple aside to add later. Add the fructose and coconut extract to the juice and mix until the fructose is thoroughly dissolved. Add the cauliflower and mix well; then add the crushed pineapple and mix well again. Cover and refrigerate for at least 2 hours before serving. (It is even better if allowed to stand several hours or overnight.) Divide evenly onto chilled plates and lightly sprinkle each serving with cinnamon. Add a sprig of mint for garnish, if available.

    This salad is named *Mystery* Slaw because many of your guests will think they are eating shredded fresh coconut and pineapple.

Variation This salad is also good with the addition of diced apples or oranges, sliced bananas, chopped mangoes or papayas, or practically any fresh fruit you desire. In fact, I sometimes add a variety of fruit and serve it in sherbet glasses as a dessert instead of a salad. You can also add drained low-sodium tuna or diced cooked chicken or turkey and serve it as a luncheon entrée.

WILTED SPANISH SALAD

1/4 cup olive oil
1/2 teaspoon ground cumin
1/4 teaspoon garlic powder
1 tablespoon fresh lemon juice
Dash Tabasco sauce
1 large head iceberg lettuce, finely shredded
  (about 8 cups)

Makes 6 servings
Each serving contains approximately:
2 fat portions
90 calories
10 mg. sodium

Combine the olive oil, cumin and garlic powder in a small saucepan and heat until hot enough to wilt the lettuce. Add the lemon juice and Tabasco sauce to the olive oil mixture. Mix well and pour over the shredded lettuce. Toss thoroughly and serve immediately.

PINK PARTY SALAD

1/4 cup sliced almonds

2 medium apples, diced

3 medium raw beets, peeled and shredded

2 cups diced unsalted farmer's cheese
   (1/2 pound)

1 large head lettuce, finely chopped (8 cups)

3/4 cup Curried Applesauce Dressing, page 63

4 red cabbage leaves

Makes 4 servings

Each serving contains approximately:

1 vegetable portion

1/2 fruit portion

4 fat portions

2 low-fat protein portions

335 calories

60 mg. sodium

Preheat the oven to 350°. Place the almonds on a cookie sheet in the preheated 350° oven for approximately 8 to 10 minutes, or until a golden brown. Watch them carefully as they burn easily. Set aside.

Combine all remaining ingredients, except the cabbage leaves, and toss well. Place the cabbage leaves on 4 chilled plates and divide the salad evenly onto the leaves. Sprinkle each salad with 1 tablespoonful of the toasted almonds.

SHADES OF GREEN SALAD

3 large cucumbers, peeled

1 tablespoon fructose

1/2 cup fresh lemon juice

1/4 cup finely chopped fresh mint

Mint sprigs for garnish

Makes 8 servings

Each serving contains approximately:

Calories negligible

3 mg. sodium

Cut the cucumbers in half lengthwise. Remove all of the seeds from each cucumber half, using a melon ball cutter or a teaspoon. Slice each cucumber half crosswise into very thin slices. Spread the cucumber slices out in a large glass baking dish and sprinkle the fructose evenly over the top. Cover and allow to stand for at least 2 hours. Drain thoroughly and set aside.

Combine the lemon juice and mint and mix thoroughly. Add the cucumber slices, again mixing thoroughly. Serve on chilled plates and garnish each serving with a sprig of fresh mint.

vegetables

Vegetables play an important role in any modified diet program because they tend to be low in calories and high in vitamins and minerals. In a low-sodium diet, however, there is an unusual paradox: Many of the vegetables lowest in calories and allowed in unlimited quantities in other diet programs are extremely high in sodium and must be restricted in the low-sodium diet. Two good examples are celery and spinach. In this chapter I have placed most of the emphasis on low-sodium vegetables, but have included a few recipes using the vegetables in the higher sodium category to show you how, if they are particular favorites, they can be incorporated *in limited amounts.* This is part of my "never say 'never'" philosophy that I mentioned in "The Low-Sodium Diet Program."

TARRAGON-CREAMED LETTUCE

1-1/2 large heads iceberg lettuce, shredded
  (about 10 cups)
2 cups low-sodium low-fat milk
1 tablespoon unsalted butter or corn oil
  margarine
2-1/2 tablespoons all-purpose flour
1/8 teaspoon white pepper
2 teaspoons dried tarragon, crushed
2 teaspoons fresh lemon juice

Makes 6 servings
Each serving contains approximately:
1/2 fat portion
1/2 low-fat milk portion
1/2 vegetable portion
99 calories
16 mg. sodium

Steam the lettuce over rapidly boiling water until just crisp tender, about 1 minute. Immediately place under cold running water to stop the cooking and to preserve the color. Drain thoroughly and set aside.

Put the milk in a saucepan on low heat. In another saucepan, melt the butter. Add the flour and cook, stirring constantly, for 3 minutes. *Do not brown.* Take the flour-butter mixture off the heat and add the hot milk all at once, stirring constantly with a wire whisk. Put the saucepan on low heat and cook slowly, stirring occasionally, for 20 to 30 minutes. Add the white pepper and tarragon and mix well. (If there are any lumps in the sauce, whirl it in a blender to smooth it.) Add the lemon juice and combine the sauce and steamed lettuce, tossing thoroughly. Serve hot or refrigerate and serve cold.

This recipe sounds a bit unusual because it *is* a bit unusual, but it is also delicious.

BROCCOLI FLOWERETS

2 pounds broccoli (4 to 6 stalks)

Makes 4 cups

1 cup contains approximately:
1 vegetable portion
25 calories
22 mg. sodium

Carefully remove each broccoli floweret from stalks, reserving the stalks for Broccoli Stars, following. Steam the flowerets over rapidly boiling water for approximately 5 to 8 minutes, or until crisp tender. Remove from the heat and place under cold running water to stop the cooking and preserve the color. Drain thoroughly and chill if using for hors d'oeuvres or in a salad. To serve hot, reheat them immediately or chill them and reheat and serve them later. When reheating vegetables prepared in this manner be careful they do not overcook or you will destroy both the crispness and the color.

BROCCOLI STARS

6 to 8 broccoli stems (1 pound)

Makes 4 cups

1/2 cup contains approximately:
1/2 vegetable portion
13 calories
11 mg. sodium

Thinly slice the broccoli stems into rounds. (You will have about 4 cups.) If you have a food processor, by all means use it, because it is difficult to slice the broccoli both thinly and evenly with a knife. When you slice across the stem you find each slice has a star pattern on it, which gives this preparation its name. Steam the "stars" over rapidly boiling water for 3 or 4 minutes, or until crisp tender. Remove them from the heat and rinse under cold running water to stop the cooking and to preserve the color. Drain thoroughly.

Broccoli Stars may be presented in a variety of ways, hot and cold. There are two recipes using them in this book—Broccoli Stars Vinaigrette and Curried Broccoli Stars. They can also either be served cold with or without a dip for a low-calorie hors d'oeuvre or mixed with other hot or cold vegetables. You will find that very few people will know what vegetable you are serving, and preparing the stems of the broccoli in this manner makes fresh broccoli a more economical vegetable. You can serve the flowerets one night and the "stars" a few nights later.

CURRIED BROCCOLI STARS

2 tablespoons unsalted butter or corn oil
  margarine
1/4 teaspoon curry powder
Dash white pepper
4 cups Broccoli Stars, preceding

Makes 4 cups
1/2 cup contains approximately:
1/2 vegetable portion
3/4 fat portion
47 calories
11 mg. sodium

Melt the butter or margarine in a large saucepan. Add the curry powder and pepper and mix thoroughly. Add the Broccoli Stars and heat thoroughly, stirring occasionally. Do not overcook or the "stars" will lose their crispness and beautiful bright green color.

MUSHROOM HORS D'OEUVRE

1 pound large fresh mushrooms (4 cups)
2 cups red wine vinegar
1/2 cup Secret Tarragon Dressing, page 59
1/4 cup minced parsley

Each whole mushroom contains
  approximately:
1/2 fat portion
23 calories
1 mg. sodium

When buying fresh mushrooms, make certain you get those with tightly closed caps. This indicates they are very fresh. When the caps are open, the mushrooms tend to be dry and tough.

Wash the mushrooms and dry them thoroughly. Slice them vertically into slices about 1/4 inch thick. Put the slices in a jar or other nonmetal container and pour the vinegar over them. If the vinegar does not cover the mushrooms, add more to cover. Cover the container and allow to stand at room temperature for 1 hour.

Remove the mushrooms from the vinegar and arrange decoratively on a large platter or serving dish. Evenly pour the Secret Tarragon Dressing over them, then sprinkle the parsley on top. Cover the platter with foil or plastic wrap and place in the refrigerator for at least 3 hours before serving.

Serve as an hors d'oeuvre with toothpicks for spearing, as a cold vegetable plate on a buffet with a salad serving fork, or as a garnish for individual salads. This amount will serve at least 24 as an hors d'oeuvre.

ARTICHOKE ROSETTES

12 tiny artichokes (or 6 large artichokes)
Fresh lemon juice or vinegar

Makes 6 servings

Each serving (artichoke only) contains
  approximately:
1 vegetable portion
25 calories
46 mg. sodium

Wash artichokes well and pull off tough outer leaves. Place in cold water to cover to which a tablespoon or so of lemon juice or vinegar has been added. Let stand for 30 minutes or more. This will force out any bugs that may be trapped between the leaves. Remove from water, and holding each artichoke by its stem, cut the tips off the leaves with scissors. When trimming the tips, start at the bottom of the artichoke and work your way to the top in a spiral pattern. Trim off the stems, even with the bottoms, turn the the artichokes upside down and press firmly to open them up as much as possible.

Pour water to a depth of 2 inches in the bottom of a saucepan and bring to a boil. Place the artichokes in the boiling water, cover tightly and cook over medium heat about 25 minutes for small artichokes or 40 minutes for large, or until stems can be easily pierced with a fork.

Remove the artichokes from the water and place upside down to drain until cool enough to handle easily. Remove the center leaves and spread the artichoke open very carefully. Reach down into the center and remove the furry choke, pulling it out a little at a time. Be sure to remove the entire choke so you will have a clean, edible artichoke bowl. (The serrated edge of a grapefruit spoon works well for scraping out the choke.)

When serving tiny artichokes, spoon a little unsalted mayonnaise into the center of each artichoke and serve as an appetizer. When serving large artichokes, place each artichoke on an artichoke plate, if you have them, or on a dinner plate, and serve unsalted mayonnaise on the side to use as a dip for the leaves.

Variation One of my favorite first courses is a large "artichoke bowl" filled with cold, jelled soup—you are then literally serving the soup in a salad. Artichoke bowls are also excellent and beautiful cold luncheon entrées filled with a chicken or seafood salad. Serve the artichoke bowl hot, filled with either rice or a different-colored, low-sodium vegetable for an unusual hot vegetable side dish. You can also fill the hot artichokes with hot fish, chicken or meat filling for an entrée.

STRING BEAN HORS D'OEUVRE

1 pound string beans

Makes about 3 cups

1 cup contains approximately:
1 vegetable portion
25 calories
6 mg. sodium

Remove the ends and strings from the beans and steam the beans over rapidly boiling water for 5 to 10 minutes, or until crisp tender. Remove from the heat and immediately place under cold running water to stop the cooking and to preserve the color. Drain thoroughly and chill before serving.

String beans prepared this way make a uniquely different hors d'oeuvre. They can also be reheated in unsalted butter or corn oil margarine and served as a hot vegetable. When reheating be careful not to overcook them or they will lose both their crispness and color.

BRUSSELS SPROUTS AL DENTE

1 pound Brussels sprouts (about 28 sprouts or
    4 cups)

Makes 4 cups

1 cup contains approximately:
1 vegetable portion
25 calories
16 mg. sodium

Cut the rough ends off the Brussels sprouts and discard any discolored outer leaves. Steam over rapidly boiling water for 10 to 15 minutes, or until crisp tender. Remove from the heat and immediately place under cold running water to stop the cooking and to preserve the color. Drain thoroughly and chill before serving.

Brussels sprouts prepared in this manner make a wonderful low-calorie hors d'oeuvre served with or without a dip. They may also be reheated and served as a hot vegetable. When reheating be careful not to overcook them or they will lose both their crispness and color.

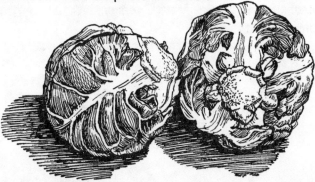

ASPARAGUS TIPS

1 pound asparagus (18 to 20 spears)

Makes 2 cups

1 cup contains approximately:
1 vegetable portion
25 calories
1 mg. sodium

Break the tough ends off each asparagus stalk by holding the stalk in both hands and gently bending the stem end until it breaks. Each stalk will break at a slightly different place depending upon its toughness. Steam the asparagus tips over rapidly boiling water for 3 to 5 minutes, or until crisp tender. Remove from the heat and immediately place under cold running water to stop the cooking and to preserve the color. Drain thoroughly.

You can use this recipe to make Asparagus Vinaigrette (following), one of my favorite appetizers that can also be served as a salad course. Cold asparagus tips make a delicious hors d'oeuvre with or without a dip, or you can reheat them and serve them as a hot vegetable. When reheating, be careful not to overcook them or they will lose both their crispness and color.

ASPARAGUS VINAIGRETTE

30 asparagus spears
1-1/2 cups Secret Vinaigrette Dressing,
    page 59
1 4-ounce jar pimientos, cut into strips

Makes 6 servings

Each serving contains approximately:
1/2 fat portion
1 vegetable portion
48 calories
2 mg. sodium

Prepare and steam the asparagus spears as directed in Asparagus Tips, preceding. After placing the asparagus under cold running water, cool to room temperature and place in a glass baking dish, pointing the tips all in the same direction (this makes removing them for serving much simpler). Pour the Secret Vinaigrette Dressing over them and cover the dish tightly with foil. Refrigerate all day or overnight.

To serve, place on chilled asparagus plates or salad plates and put pimiento strips evenly over each serving. I often serve this as a first course, omitting salad.

BROWN ONIONS

2-1/2 pounds onions (4 large)
1 teaspoon corn oil

Makes about 2 cups
1/2 cup contains approximately:

1 vegetable portion
1/4 fat portion
36 calories
9 mg. sodium

Peel the onions and slice them very thinly. Pour the corn oil into a cured heavy iron skillet. Using a paper towel, wipe the oil over the entire inner surface of the skillet. Put the skillet on medium heat and add the onions. Cook, stirring frequently, for 30 minutes. Reduce heat to low and continue cooking, stirring occasionally, for another 30 minutes, or a little longer if necessary to lightly brown the onions.

You can, of course, use less onions. I generally cook at least 4, and store any left over in the refrigerator. I can then quickly reheat them to use as a garnish on steaks, chops, meat patties, or even chicken.

DILLED ONION RELISH

1 cup distilled white vinegar
3/4 cup fructose
1 tablespoon dried dill weed, crushed
1/4 cup water
4 large white onions, finely chopped
1 green bell pepper, seeded and finely chopped
1 4-ounce jar pimientos, finely chopped

Makes 4-1/2 cups
1/2 cup contains approximately:
1 vegetable portion
1 fruit portion
65 calories
10 mg. sodium

Combine the vinegar and fructose in a small bowl and stir until the fructose is completely dissolved. Add the dill weed and water and mix well. Place the onions, green pepper and pimiento together in a jar and pour the liquid over them. Cover with a tight-fitting lid and shake the jar until the ingredients are thoroughly mixed. Refrigerate for 2 days before serving.

Dilled Onion Relish is good with cold meats, fish, poultry, in salads, on sandwiches—use your imagination.

MARINATED ZUCCHINI SPEARS

6 medium zucchini, cut into quarters
   lengthwise
1/4 cup fresh lemon juice
1-1/2 cups Secret Cumin Dressing, page 60
1 large ripe tomato, peeled and diced
1 large onion, diced
1 cup finely minced parsley

Makes 8 servings
Each serving contains approximately:
1 vegetable portion
1/2 fat portion
48 calories
8 mg. sodium

Place the zucchini quarters in a glass baking dish and pour the lemon juice evenly over them. Cover and allow to stand for at least 1 hour. Pour off the liquid. Place the zucchini over rapidly boiling water and steam about 2 to 3 minutes, or until just crisp tender. Put the zucchini back in the glass baking dish, pour the dressing over, and allow the zucchini to cool to room temperature. Sprinkle the tomato and onion on top, cover and chill for at least 3 hours before serving.

    Divide evenly onto chilled plates and sprinkle parsley over each serving. This can be served as an appetizer, salad or cold vegetable side dish.

ZUCCHINI IN BASIL BUTTER

4 large zucchini, sliced on the diagonal
3 tablespoons unsalted butter or corn oil
   margarine
2 teaspoons dried basil, crushed
1/4 teaspoon Tabasco sauce

Makes 8 servings
Each serving contains approximately:
1 vegetable portion
1 fat portion
70 calories
2 mg. sodium

Steam the zucchini over rapidly boiling water about 2 to 3 minutes, or until just crisp tender. Remove from the heat and immediately place under cold running water to stop the cooking and to preserve the color. Drain thoroughly.

Heat the butter or margarine in a skillet and add the basil. Place the steamed zucchini in the basil butter and heat to serving temperature.

This is a simple and delicious vegetable side dish. It may also be combined with fish, poultry or meat as an entrée.

Variation I have used zucchini because I particularly like it with basil. Broccoli, asparagus or Brussels sprouts would, however, also be good.

CURRIED ZUCCHINI PURÉE

1/2 cup water
1 teaspoon fructose
2 pounds zucchini, sliced (4 medium or
   6 cups, sliced)
1 large onion, chopped
1 cup low-sodium low-fat milk
2 teaspoons unsalted butter or corn oil
   margarine
1 tablespoon all-purpose flour
1 teaspoon curry powder

1/4 teaspoon ground ginger
2 teaspoons fresh lemon juice

Makes 4 cups
1/2 cup contains approximately:
1 vegetable portion
1/4 fat portion
36 calories
10 mg. sodium

Combine the water and fructose in a large saucepan and bring to a boil. Add the zucchini and onion, cover, reduce heat and simmer until just tender, about 5 minutes. Put the zucchini-onion mixture and all of its liquid in a blender container and blend until smooth; set aside.

Put the milk in a saucepan on low heat. In another saucepan, melt the butter or margarine. Add the flour and cook, stirring constantly, for 3 minutes. *Do not brown.* Remove from the heat and add the simmering milk all at once, stirring constantly with a wire whisk. Add the curry powder and ginger to the sauce and mix well. Put the saucepan on low heat and cook, stirring occasionally, for 20 minutes. Remove from the heat. Add the lemon juice and the puréed zucchini-onion mixture to the sauce and mix well. Heat to desired temperature before serving.

Puréed vegetables are a nice change on occasion, and this recipe is one of my favorites. If you have any left over, chill it and use it as a low-calorie dip for other raw or cold cooked vegetables. In fact, I sometimes make this recipe and use it as a dip at parties.

CHINESE PEA PODS AND WATER CHESTNUTS

4 teaspoons corn oil
2 teaspoons grated ginger root, or
   1/4 teaspoon ground ginger
3/4 pound pea pods (snow peas)
1/4 cup sherry
2 teaspoons fresh lemon juice
1 6-ounce can water chestnuts, drained
   and very thinly sliced

Makes 8 servings
Each serving contains approximately:
1/2 fat portion
1-1/2 vegetable portions
61 calories
4 mg. sodium

Heat the corn oil in a large skillet or wok. Add the ginger and stir a few seconds. Add the pea pods and cook over low heat, stirring constantly, for 3 to 5 minutes, or until crisp tender. Add the sherry, lemon juice and water chestnuts and cook, stirring constantly, for 2 more minutes. Serve immediately.

   I like to serve this dish as an accompaniment to Cantonese Sweet and Sour Pork. If there are any leftovers, refrigerate them and add them to a salad on the following day.

BAKED PARSLEY

4 cups coarsely chopped parsley
2 quarts water
1 tablespoon fructose

1/2 cup contains approximately:
1/2 vegetable portion
13 calories
32 mg. sodium

Makes 2 cups

Combine the parsley, water and fructose in a large container and allow to stand for 1 hour. Preheat the oven to 350°. Thoroughly drain the parsley and spread it evenly in a large baking dish. Bake in the preheated 350° oven for approximately 25 minutes or until crisp.

   This is a delightfully different vegetable dish. Eating it is much like eating cotton candy—when you start to chew, as if by magic it is gone. It also makes a lovely low-calorie topping for other vegetables and for soups, salads, fish, poultry and meats. Soaking the parsley in the fructose water before baking adds flavor.

SAVORY TOMATOES AU GRATIN

4 large ripe tomatoes
1/2 cup low-sodium low-fat milk
1 teaspoon fresh lemon juice
2 teaspoons dried summer savory, crushed
1/2 cup grated low-sodium cheddar cheese

Makes 8 servings
Each tomato half contains approximately:
3/4 vegetable portion
1/4 high-fat protein portion
43 calories
8 mg. sodium

Preheat the oven to 400°. Cut the tomatoes in half, remove the seeds and place the halves, cut side up, in a shallow flameproof dish. Combine the milk and lemon juice and drizzle 1 tablespoon of the mixture onto each tomato half. Sprinkle 1/4 teaspoon of summer savory evenly over each tomato half, then 1 tablespoon of the grated cheese. Put the tomatoes in the preheated 400° oven for 15 minutes. Remove from the oven and place under the broiler until lightly browned.

This is an excellent accompaniment to fish, poultry and meat, or to omelets for brunch. If you wish, add more cheese and make it a vegetarian entrée.

OPEN-FACED B.L.T.
(bacon-flavored lettuce and tomato sandwich)

1/4 cup Unsalted Mayonnaise, page 52
1 tablespoon Bakon Yeast
4 slices low-sodium whole wheat bread,
    toasted
2 medium ripe tomatoes, thinly sliced
Freshly ground black pepper
4 large lettuce leaves
Parsley sprigs for garnish

Makes 4 servings
Each serving contains approximately:
1 starch portion
1/2 vegetable portion
3 fat portions
218 calories
24 mg. sodium

Combine the mayonnaise and Bakon Yeast and mix well. Spread 1 tablespoon of the mayonnaise mixture evenly on each slice of toast. Arrange all but 4 of the tomato slices evenly on the 4 slices of toast. Sprinkle each sandwich lightly with pepper and place a lettuce leaf on top of each sandwich. Top the lettuce with the reserved tomato slices and place each sandwich on a plate. Garnish with parsley sprigs.

Serve this modified classic to your salt-loving friends and amaze them with the taste.

BAKED SPAGHETTI SQUASH

1 spaghetti squash

1 cup contains approximately:

1 vegetable portion
25 calories
2 mg. sodium

Preheat the oven to 350°. Cut the squash in half with a heavy knife and remove and discard the seeds. (You may cut it crosswise or lengthwise; the latter will give you longer strands.) Place the halves, cut side down, in a baking dish. Bake in the preheated 350° oven for about 1 hour, or until fork tender. Remove from the oven and pull the cooked flesh in strands from the skin with a fork.

This unusual vegetable looks very much like spaghetti, but has only about one-fifth the calories. It contains more calories than either summer squash or zucchini, but only half the calories of winter squash, such as Hubbard and acorn. I like to use spaghetti squash for making the Vegetarian Spaghetti Variation, which follows, or serve it buttered and seasoned as you like.

VEGETARIAN SPAGHETTI

4 quarts water
1/2 teaspoon garlic powder
1 teaspoon fresh lemon juice
1 tablespoon olive oil
1 pound spaghetti
6 cups Marinara Sauce, page 48, heated to
   serving temperature
1/4 cup freshly grated Parmesan cheese
1/4 cup low-sodium bread crumbs, toasted

Makes 8 servings
Each serving contains approximately:
2-1/4 starch portions
1 fat portion
3 vegetable portions
278 calories
97 mg. sodium

Bring the water to a boil in a large saucepan or soup kettle. Add the garlic powder, lemon juice and olive oil and boil for 5 minutes. Add the spaghetti and cook for about 8 to 10 minutes, or until al dente (meaning it has a slight resilience when eaten). Drain well and toss with the Marinara Sauce. Combine the Parmesan cheese and toasted bread crumbs, mix well and sprinkle 1 tablespoon of the mixture over each serving.

Variation Substitute 6 cups Baked Spaghetti Squash, preceding, for the spaghetti and combine with the Marinara Sauce. Sprinkle with the Parmesan cheese-bread crumb mixture, following the instructions for Vegetarian Spaghetti. Each serving will contain approximately 1 fat portion, 4 vegetable portions, 145 calories and 96 mg. sodium.

CARAWAY CABBAGE

2 tablespoons unsalted butter or corn oil
   margarine
1 large head white cabbage, finely shredded
1-1/2 teaspoons caraway seeds

Makes 8 servings

Each serving contains approximately:
1 vegetable portion
3/4 fat portion
59 calories
16 mg. sodium

Melt the butter or margarine in a large skillet. Add the cabbage and cook, stirring frequently, 10 to 15 minutes, or until crisp tender. Remove from the heat, add the caraway seeds and mix thoroughly. Serve immediately, or refrigerate and serve cold.

VEGETARIAN TURKEY DRESSING

1/2 cup finely chopped almonds
2 eggs, lightly beaten
1 teaspoon dried marjoram, crushed
1/2 teaspoon dried sage, crushed
1/2 teaspoon dried thyme, crushed
1 medium eggplant, unpeeled and diced
2 large onions, finely chopped
2 large red apples, cored and diced
1 cup finely chopped parsley

Makes 8 servings
Each serving contains approximately:
1-1/2 vegetable portions
1/4 medium-fat protein portion
1/4 fruit portion
1/2 fat portion
90 calories
25 mg. sodium

Preheat the oven to 350°. Place the almonds on a cookie sheet in the preheated oven for 8 to 10 minutes, or until a golden brown. Watch them carefully as they burn easily. Set aside.

Combine the eggs, marjoram, sage and thyme and mix thoroughly in a large mixing bowl. Add all other ingredients, except the almonds, to the egg mixture and again mix thoroughly. Place in a casserole and bake, covered, in the preheated 350° oven for 1 hour. Just before serving, combine the toasted almonds with the dressing and mix well or, alternately, sprinkle the almonds over the top of each serving.

EGGPLANT PIZZA

1 large firm eggplant
1/4 cup fresh lemon juice
2 cups unsalted tomato juice (1 16-ounce can)
2 tablespoons red wine vinegar
1 medium onion, finely chopped
1-1/2 teaspoons dried oregano, crushed
1 tablespoon olive oil
Freshly ground black pepper
1 cup grated low-sodium Swiss-type cheese

Makes 8 servings
Each serving contains approximately:
1/4 fat portion
1-1/2 vegetable portions
1/2 high-fat protein portion
97 calories
23 mg. sodium

Peel the eggplant and slice it crosswise into 1/4-inch-thick slices. Spread the eggplant slices in a glass baking dish and sprinkle both sides with fresh lemon juice. Cover and allow to stand for at least 1 hour. Pour off the liquid.

While the eggplant is marinating, put the tomato juice in a large saucepan. Add the vinegar and onion and bring to a boil. Simmer, uncovered, for 1 hour. Add the oregano and continue to simmer for 30 more minutes.

Preheat the oven to 400°. Heat the olive oil in a large skillet. Sprinkle each slice of drained eggplant with pepper and sauté in the hot oil until fork tender and golden brown on both sides. Place the cooked eggplant in a large flameproof baking dish. Spread the tomato sauce evenly over the eggplant and place it in the preheated 400° oven for 10 minutes. Remove from the oven and sprinkle the grated cheese evenly over the top of the eggplant. Place under the broiler until the cheese is melted and lightly browned.

EGGPLANT SUBLIME

2 medium eggplants, unpeeled
2 tablespoons corn oil
2 16-ounce cans unsalted tomatoes, with
   juice
1 cup water
1/2 cup red wine vinegar
1 teaspoon ground coriander
1 teaspoon dried sage, crushed
1/2 teaspoon dried thyme, crushed
1/2 teaspoon dried rosemary, crushed
1/2 teaspoon cracked black pepper
2 large garlic buds, pressed

1/2 lemon, sliced (with peel)
1 large green bell pepper, seeded and thinly
   sliced
1 large onion, thinly sliced
1 tablespoon fructose

Makes 12 servings
Each serving contains approximately:
1-1/2 vegetable portions
1/2 fat portion
61 calories
15 mg. sodium

Trim stems off eggplants and cut eggplants crosswise into 1/4-inch-thick slices. Heat the corn oil in a large heavy skillet and sauté eggplant slices on both sides until lightly browned; set aside.

Preheat the oven to 350°. In a large saucepan, combine the tomatoes and their juice with all remaining ingredients. Bring to a boil and simmer, uncovered, until reduced by half. Make a layer of the eggplant in the bottom of a casserole. Top with some of the sauce. Repeat layers until all ingredients are used, ending with sauce. Cover the casserole with a lid or aluminum foil and bake in the preheated 350° oven for 1 hour.

PORTUGUESE PILAF

3 tablespoons corn oil
2 garlic buds, minced
1 cup long-grain white rice
1 medium onion, thinly sliced
2 cups Unsalted Chicken Stock, page 34, boiling
1 teaspoon dried oregano, crushed
1/2 teaspoon chili powder
1/2 teaspoon ground cumin

1/4 teaspoon freshly ground black pepper
1/8 teaspoon Tabasco sauce

Makes 12 servings
Each serving (1/2 cup) contains approximately:
1 starch portion
3/4 fat portion
104 calories
8 mg. sodium

Preheat the oven to 400°. Heat the corn oil in a cured heavy iron skillet. Add the garlic, rice and onion and cook, stirring frequently, until browned. Combine the hot chicken stock with all remaining ingredients and mix well. Put the rice mixture in a casserole dish with a tight-fitting lid. Add the hot stock mixture and mix well. Cover and place in the preheated 400° oven for 40 minutes. Remove from the oven and allow to stand, covered, for 10 minutes before serving.

Note If you wish to reheat the pilaf, add 2 or 3 tablespoons of Unsalted Chicken Stock to the cold rice and mix thoroughly. Cover and heat in a preheated 300° for about 30 minutes.

SOUTHERN YAM CASSEROLE

2 cups mashed cooked yams
3/4 cup low-sodium low-fat milk
1/2 cup fresh orange juice
1 tablespoon freshly grated orange peel
1/2 teaspoon ground nutmeg
1/4 cup fructose
4 eggs, beaten

Makes 8 servings
Each serving contains approximately:
1 starch portion
1/2 fruit portion
1/2 medium-fat protein portion
128 calories
38 mg. sodium

Preheat the oven to 350°. Combine the yams, milk, orange juice, orange peel, nutmeg and fructose and mix well. Add the beaten eggs and mix well again. Pour into a casserole and bake, uncovered, in the preheated 350° oven for approximately 45 minutes.

WILD RICE À L'ORANGE

3/4 cup raw wild rice (4 ounces)
2 cups Unsalted Chicken Stock, page 34
2 tablespoons freshly grated orange peel
1 teaspoon dried thyme, crushed
1/2 cup chopped almonds
1 tablespoon unsalted butter or corn oil
   margarine

Makes 6 servings
Each serving (1/2 cup) contains
  approximately:
1 starch portion
1-1/2 fat portions
138 calories
9 mg. sodium

Combine the wild rice, chicken stock, orange peel and thyme in a saucepan with a lid. Bring to a boil, reduce heat, cover and simmer about 35 minutes or until all liquid is absorbed and the rice is fluffy. Remove from the heat and set aside.

    While the rice is cooking, preheat the oven to 350°. Place the almonds on a cookie sheet in the preheated oven for about 8 to 10 minutes, or until a golden brown. Watch them carefully as they burn easily. Combine the cooked rice, toasted almonds and butter or margarine and mix thoroughly.

B & B POTATO BOATS
(baked and broiled)

3 large baking potatoes
Corn oil
1 large onion, thinly sliced
2 tablespoons unsalted butter or corn oil
   margarine
1/3 cup low-sodium low-fat milk
1/4 teaspoon white pepper
1/2 teaspoon onion powder
1/2 teaspoon liquid smoke

1 tablespoon grated Parmesan cheese
Paprika for garnish

Makes 6 servings
Each serving contains approximately:
1 starch portion
1 fat portion
115 calories
13 mg. sodium

Preheat the oven to 400°. Thoroughly scrub the potatoes so that the skins are clean enough to eat. Rub the outside of each potato with corn oil. Cut each in half lengthwise and evenly divide the onion slices between the 6 potato halves. Put each potato back together again with the onion slices between the halves and wrap tightly with aluminum foil. Put the potatoes in a baking dish or on a cookie sheet, place in the center of the preheated 400° oven and bake for 1 hour.

Remove the potatoes from the oven and unwrap them. Remove the onions and put them in a large mixing bowl. Carefully scoop the cooked potato from each potato half so as not to tear the skin and add the potato to the onion. Reserve the 6 potato skins to use as "boats." Add the butter or margarine to the potatoes and onions. Combine the milk with the white pepper, onion powder and liquid smoke, mix well and add to the potato mixture. Using an electric mixer or a whisk, whip the potato mixture until it is thoroughly mixed and smooth in texture. Divide the potato mixture evenly into the 6 "boats" and sprinkle 1/2 teaspoon of Parmesan cheese on top of each serving. Sprinkle a little paprika over the top for garnish. Place the potatoes under the broiler until they are lightly browned.

BAKED BEANS

1 pound dried pinto beans (2-1/2 cups)
6 cups water
2 large onions, finely chopped
4 garlic buds, minced
2 bay leaves
1 16-ounce can unsalted tomatoes, with
   juice
1/2 cup fructose
1 tablespoon chili powder
1 teaspoon dry mustard
1 teaspoon dried oregano, crushed

1 tablespoon liquid smoke
1/4 cup red wine vinegar

Makes 10 servings
Each serving (1/2 cup) contains
   approximately:
1 starch portion
1 vegetable portion
3/4 fruit portion
125 calories
24 mg. sodium

Soak the beans overnight in the water. The next day, add the onions, garlic and bay leaves to the beans and water and bring to a boil. Reduce heat, cover and simmer for 1-1/2 hours or until beans are tender.

Preheat the oven to 350°. Combine the beans and all remaining ingredients in a 7- by 12-inch baking dish. Bake in the preheated 350° oven for 1 hour or until the liquid is absorbed.

eggs and cheese

In all of the recipes in this section, egg substitutes may be used in place of eggs if you are trying to lower cholesterol as well as sodium. The sodium figures for each recipe are based on one medium egg equaling 59 milligrams sodium. Because this same egg contains 250 milligrams of cholesterol, you may wish to use egg substitutes and use your cholesterol allotment elsewhere in your diet program.

Many cheeses are not only high in sodium, but are also high in cholesterol, so you will have to check package figures very carefully. Unfortunately, all low-sodium cheese brands are not available in all geographical areas, making it impossible to specify exact types or brands of cheese in the following recipes. I simply give low-sodium cheese as an ingredient and use the average number of milligrams per ounce for most low-sodium cheeses in figuring the sodium present in each serving.

Commercial cottage cheese is very high in sodium because salt is added to the cottage cheese before packaging. In some areas it is difficult to find low-sodium cottage cheese. For this reason I have supplied two recipes, one an instant approach and the other an overnight version, for making your own cottage cheese. I have been making my own cottage cheese for so long while working on this book that I have actually come to prefer it over anything I can buy.

POACHED EGGS

2 quarts water
2 tablespoons distilled white vinegar
1 tablespoon fresh lemon juice
Eggs, as desired

Each egg contains approximately:
1 medium-fat protein portion
75 calories
59 mg. sodium

Put the water, vinegar and lemon juice in a large pan and bring to a boil. When the water is boiling, break each egg into a saucer, one at a time, and slide it into the water, working quickly so that they cook evenly. Turn the heat down to simmer and poach the eggs about 2 to 3 minutes, depending on how firm you want them. Do not put too many eggs into the pan at once, as they are difficult to handle. Remove the eggs from the water with a slotted spoon and dip each egg into a bowl of warm water to rinse it. Then blot with a paper towel before serving.

Poached eggs may be made ahead of serving time and stored in the refrigerator. In order to store the eggs after poaching them, put them directly in a bowl of ice water. To reheat them, put the eggs in a large pan of warm water with a little salt and bring the water almost to a boil. Remove each egg and blot with a paper towel before serving.

BASIC OMELET

2 eggs
Dash white pepper
Dash freshly ground black pepper
2 teaspoons water
1 teaspoon fresh lemon juice
1/2 teaspoon unsalted butter or corn oil
   margarine

Makes 1 serving
Each serving contains approximately:
2 medium-fat protein portions
1/2 fat portion
173 calories
118 mg. sodium

Beat the eggs with a fork or wire whisk until frothy. Add all remaining ingredients, except the butter or margarine, and beat again. Melt the butter or margarine in a 10-inch omelet pan or round-bottom skillet until very hot. Reduce the heat and pour in the beaten egg mixture. Tilt the pan so that the liquid covers most of its inner surface. Using a fork, lift the edges of the omelet, tilting the pan as you do it so that the liquid from the center runs underneath to cook. When the bottom is cooked and the top is still a bit runny, fold one-third of the omelet toward the center. Rest the edge of the pan on a plate and quickly turn the pan upside down so the omelet slides out on the plate folded in thirds.

Note You can, of course, fill your omelet with any filling you desire. What you use for filling should be ready when you pour the beaten egg into the pan. Then, before folding the omelet, put the filling in a strip in the center and fold as directed.

PEACHES 'N' CREAM OMELET

1/4 cup sour cream
2 teaspoons fructose
1/4 teaspoon vanilla extract
2 eggs
2 teaspoons water
1 teaspoon fresh lemon juice
1/2 teaspoon unsalted butter or corn oil
   margarine
1 small peach, peeled and diced

Ground cinnamon for garnish

Makes 1 serving
Each serving contains approximately:
2 medium-fat protein portions
2-1/2 fat portions
1 fruit portion
303 calories
143 mg. sodium

Combine the sour cream, 1 teaspoon of the fructose and the vanilla extract and mix well; set aside. Beat the eggs with a fork or wire whisk until frothy. Add the remaining teaspoon fructose, the water and lemon juice and beat again. Melt the butter or margarine in a 10-inch omelet pan or round-bottom skillet until very hot and cook the egg mixture according to directions in Basic Omelet, preceding. Spoon the diced peaches in a strip down the center before folding. Once the omelet is on the plate, spoon the sour cream mixture over it and sprinkle a little cinnamon on top.

This omelet may also be made with other fresh fruit or berries in season, or with canned peaches packed either in water or natural juice without added sugar or salt. It may also be served for a dessert, but halve the serving size.

CHEESE AND CHIVE OMELET

2 eggs
Dash white pepper
1/2 teaspoon liquid smoke
1 tablespoon water
1/4 cup chopped chives
1/2 teaspoon unsalted butter or corn oil
   margarine
1/4 cup grated low-sodium cheese

Makes 1 serving
Each serving contains approximately:
2 medium-fat protein portions
1 high-fat protein portion
1/2 fat portion
268 calories
132 mg. sodium

Put the eggs, pepper, liquid smoke, water and chives in a blender container and blend until frothy. Melt the butter or margarine in a 10-inch omelet pan or round-bottom skillet until very hot and cook the egg mixture according to directions for Basic Omelet, page 96. Sprinkle the cheese in a strip down the center before folding and proceed as directed.

LEFTOVER OMELET

Use leftover cooked vegetables, cold fish, poultry or meat, casserole dishes, sauces, even desserts to fill your omelets. Use your imagination. Calculate your own food portions, calories and sodium content using the charts at the front of the book. Leftover Omelets are my favorite Sunday brunch entrée. In fact, my children call them "clean the refrigerator specials," since sometimes each person's omelet contains a different leftover.

SOUFFLÉ SANS SEL

1 cup low-sodium low-fat milk
2 tablespoons unsalted butter or corn oil
   margarine
1/2 teaspoon onion powder
2-1/2 tablespoons all-purpose flour
3 egg yolks
1 teaspoon fresh lemon juice
1/8 teaspoon white pepper
Dash Tabasco sauce
1/2 cup grated low-sodium cheddar cheese
5 egg whites, at room temperature

1/4 teaspoon cream of tartar

Makes 4 servings
Each serving contains approximately:
1 medium-fat protein portion
1/2 high-fat protein portion
1 fat portion
1/4 starch portion
1/4 low-fat milk portion
217 calories
77 mg. sodium

Preheat the oven to 400°. Put the milk in a saucepan on low heat and bring just to the boiling point. Melt the butter or margarine in another large saucepan, add the onion powder and flour and cook, stirring constantly, for 3 minutes. *Do not brown.* Remove from the heat and pour in the hot milk all at once, stirring with a wire whisk. Put the pan back on the heat and allow to come to a boil, stirring constantly. Boil for 1 minute. At this point the sauce will be quite thick. Remove from heat. Add the egg yolks, one at a time, stirring each one in thoroughly with a wire whisk. Mix in the lemon juice, white pepper and Tabasco.

(You can make this much of a soufflé ahead of time, cover the saucepan and set it aside. Then just reheat the mixture to lukewarm before continuing. Or you can go right ahead and finish the soufflé; it will be ready 20 to 25 minutes later.)

Now add the cheese to the sauce and stir well. Put the egg whites in a large mixing bowl and add the cream of tartar. Beat the whites until stiff but not dry. Stir one-fourth of the egg whites into the cheese sauce. Add the remaining three-fourths of the whites to the cheese sauce, folding them in very carefully; be careful not to overmix. Pour the mixture into an 8-inch soufflé dish and place it in the center of the preheated 400° oven. Immediately turn the oven down to 375° and cook the soufflé 20 to 25 minutes. Serve immediately.

EGGS BENEDICT

4 teaspoons unsalted butter or corn oil
  margarine
1 teaspoon Bakon Yeast
4 thin slices cooked turkey breast meat
2 English Muffins, page 142, split and toasted
3/4 cup Hollandaise Sauce Sans Sel, page 50
4 Poached Eggs, page 95
Paprika for garnish (optional)

Makes 4 servings
Each serving contains approximately:
2 medium-fat protein portions
1 starch portion
3-1/4 fat portions
366 calories
110 mg. sodium

Melt the butter or margarine in a skillet. Add the Bakon Yeast and mix thoroughly. Place the turkey slices in the skillet and heat, turning frequently, until lightly browned on both sides. While the turkey slices are browning, spread 1 tablespoon of the hollandaise on each toasted muffin half. Place a turkey slice on top of each, then place a poached egg on top of each turkey slice. Spoon 2 tablespoons of the hollandaise on top of each serving and sprinkle on a little paprika, if desired.

This dish is a fabulous fake. The Bakon Yeast flavors the turkey slices so that they taste very much like the more classically used Canadian bacon, which is high in sodium. Serve as a brunch entrée for friends on low-sodium diets who have been unable to eat eggs Benedict for a long time.

COTTAGE CHEESE CRÊPES

2 cups (double recipe) Instant Cottage Cheese or Overnight Cottage Cheese, following
1/4 cup grated low-sodium Jack cheese
2 tablespoons grated onion
1 tablespoon finely chopped parsley
1 tablespoon finely chopped chives
1/4 teaspoon garlic powder
6 Crêpes, page 148, warmed

2 tablespoons grated Parmesan cheese

Makes 6 servings
Each serving contains approximately:
1-1/2 medium-fat protein portions
3/4 starch portion
166 calories
250 mg. sodium

Preheat the oven to 350°. Place cottage cheese in a large mixing bowl and add all remaining ingredients, except the crêpes and Parmesan cheese. Mix thoroughly. Spoon the cheese mixture evenly down the center of each warm crêpe. Fold the crêpe over the filling and place each crêpe, seam side down, in a glass baking dish. Sprinkle the Parmesan cheese evenly over the top of the crêpes and bake in a 350° oven for 20 minutes, or until the Parmesan cheese is lightly browned.

Note You may use commercial low-fat cottage cheese for this recipe. Rinse according to directions on page 178 before proceeding with method.

INSTANT COTTAGE CHEESE

1 quart low-sodium low-fat milk
1/4 cup fresh lemon juice
Additional 2 tablespoons low-sodium low-fat milk
1/8 teaspoon fructose

Makes 1 cup
1/2 cup contains approximately:
1 low-fat protein portion
55 calories
26 mg. sodium

Put the milk in a saucepan and heat to lukewarm. Remove from the heat and add the lemon juice, mix well and let stand. When the liquid portion, or whey, separates completely from the curd, line a colander with cheesecloth and strain the mixture through it. Squeeze the cheesecloth to force out any remaining liquid in the curd and place the curd in a mixing bowl. Add the 2 additional tablespoons milk and the fructose and mix well, using a wire whisk. Store in the refrigerator.

This is delicious, easy-to-make, low-sodium cottage cheese. It can be used as a base for dips, sauces and dressings, seasoned with chopped chives or served with fresh fruit.

OVERNIGHT COTTAGE CHEESE

1 quart low-sodium low-fat milk
2 tablespoons sour cream

Makes 1 cup

1/2 cup contains approximately:
1 low-fat protein portion
55 calories
31 mg. sodium

Put the milk in a glass container with a lid. Place in a warm spot until the curds (solids) have completely separated from the whey (liquid). Line a colander with cheesecloth and pour the curds and whey into it. Squeeze the curds to force out any remaining liquid. Place the curds in a mixing bowl, add the sour cream and beat with a wire whisk until smooth and creamy. Store in the refrigerator.

This cottage cheese takes longer to make than the preceding recipe using lemon juice; however, when the time is available, I prefer this one because I like the flavor and texture better.

HUEVOS RANCHEROS

1 tablespoon corn oil
1 onion, finely chopped
1 green bell pepper, seeded and finely
  chopped
3 garlic buds, minced
2 16-ounce cans unsalted tomatoes, chopped,
  with juice (4 cups)
4 green chili peppers, seeded, deveined and
  chopped
1/2 teaspoon freshly ground black pepper
2 teaspoons chili powder
2 teaspoons dried oregano, crushed
1/2 teaspoon ground cumin

6 eggs, at room temperature
1-1/2 cups grated low-sodium cheddar cheese
6 corn tortillas, warmed

Makes 6 servings
Each serving contains approximately:
1 high-fat protein portion
1 medium-fat protein portion
1/2 fat portion
1 vegetable portion
218 calories
102 mg. sodium

Heat the corn oil in a large skillet. Add the onion, bell pepper and garlic and cook until the onion is clear. Add all remaining ingredients, except the eggs, cheese and tortillas, and cook, uncovered, for 20 minutes.

Make 6 small depressions in the sauce with the back of a spoon and carefully break an egg into each depression. Sprinkle the cheese over all. Cover and cook for 3 to 5 minutes, or until the egg whites are opaque and the cheese is melted. Serve each egg on top of a hot tortilla, spooning the sauce remaining in the pan over the top of each serving.

MATZO BALLS AU GRATIN

2 cups low-sodium low-fat milk
1 tablespoon unsalted butter or corn oil
   margarine
3 tablespoons all-purpose flour
1/4 teaspoon white pepper
1/2 teaspoon dry mustard
1/2 cup grated low-sodium cheddar cheese
12 Matzo Balls, page 151

Makes 4 servings
Each serving contains approximately:
1-1/2 starch portions
3/4 fat portion
1/2 high-fat protein portion
1/2 low-fat milk portion
250 calories
42 mg. sodium

Put the milk in a saucepan on low heat and bring just to the boiling point. In another saucepan melt the butter or margarine, add the flour and cook, stirring constantly, 3 minutes. *Do not brown.* Remove from heat and add hot milk all at once, stirring constantly with a wire whisk. Add the pepper, mustard and cheese and mix well. Put the sauce back on the heat and cook slowly for 30 minutes, stirring occasionally.

   Preheat the oven to 350°. Put the Matzo Balls in a flat baking dish or 4 individual au gratin dishes and pour the cheese sauce over them. Bake in the preheated 350° oven for 30 minutes or until the cheese is lightly browned. Or bake them for 20 minutes and then place them under the broiler to lightly brown the cheese sauce before serving.

FRENCH TOAST

1/2 cup low-sodium low-fat milk
1/2 teaspoon fresh lemon juice
3 eggs, beaten
6 slices French Bread, page 135
1 tablespoon unsalted butter or corn oil
   margarine

Makes 6 servings
Each serving contains approximately:
1 starch portion
1/2 medium-fat protein portion
1/2 fat portion
131 calories
38 mg. sodium

Combine the milk and lemon juice, mixing well, and add to the eggs; beat until frothy. Dip each slice of bread in the mixture, turning it over to soak up the liquid. Heat the butter or margarine in a large skillet and cook the egg-soaked bread until lightly browned on both sides. Serve with Honey Butter, date butter or fresh fruit jam.

seafood

Fish is probably the best source of protein containing the least amount of fat, and most fish is not excessively high in sodium. If you think that you do not like fish, chances are you have never had really fresh fish or that you have always had fish overcooked to the point where it was dry and tasteless.

If possible, find a good source of fresh fish near where you live. If it is not possible to buy fresh fish, buy good fresh-frozen fish and let it thaw completely before cooking it. To avoid a "fishy" taste that many people find objectionable, first wash the fish with cold water and pat dry. Then cover it with fresh lemon juice and refrigerate it for several hours before cooking it. Marinating it in the lemon juice also reduces the need for salt in its preparation.

Shellfish tend to be higher in sodium and therefore must be used more sparingly in a low-sodium diet.

FILLET OF SOLE A LA WALNUT

8 small sole fillets (2 pounds)
2 lemons
1/2 cup finely chopped walnuts
4 tablespoons unsalted butter or corn oil
   margarine

Makes 8 servings
Each serving contains approximately:
2 low-fat protein portions
2 fat portions
200 calories
105 mg. sodium

Wash the fish in cold water and pat dry. Place the fish fillets in a flat glass baking dish and squeeze the juice of 1 lemon evenly over the top. Turn the fish over and squeeze the juice of the remaining lemon over the top. Cover and refrigerate for at least 2 hours or until you are ready to cook it.

Preheat the oven to 350°. Put the walnuts on a cookie sheet in the preheated 350° oven for 8 to 10 minutes, or until golden brown. Watch them carefully as they burn easily.

Melt 2 tablespoons of the butter or margarine in a large skillet and add 1/4 cup of the toasted walnuts. Place the fish fillets in the skillet and sauté on both sides until just done, about 10 minutes or until the fish is completely white. Remove the fish from the skillet and place it on individual plates or on a serving platter. Melt the remaining 2 tablespoons butter or margarine in the same skillet and mix in the remaining 1/4 cup toasted walnuts. Spoon the walnut mixture over the top of the cooked fish and serve.

FISH FILLETS VERONIQUE

2 pounds white fish fillets, preferably
   sea bass or red snapper
2 lemons
White pepper
1/4 cup dry white wine
2 cups seedless green grapes
2 tablespoons arrowroot
1 tablespoon fructose
2 tablespoons water
1/2 teaspoon dried tarragon, crushed
3/4 cup Unsalted White Sauce, page 49,
   heated to serving temperature

Makes 8 servings
Each serving contains approximately:
2 low-fat protein portions
3/4 fruit portion
1/4 fat portion
1/4 starch portion
169 calories
103 mg. sodium

Wash the fish in cold water and pat dry. Place the fish fillets in a flat glass baking dish, squeeze the juice of 1 lemon on the fish and sprinkle with white pepper. Turn the fish over and squeeze the juice of the remaining lemon on it. Again, lightly sprinkle the fish with white pepper. Cover the dish tightly with aluminum foil or a lid and refrigerate at least 2 hours or until 30 minutes before you plan to cook it.

Preheat the oven to 350°. Pour the wine over the fish and again cover the baking dish tightly with aluminum foil. Place it in the preheated 350° oven for about 20 minutes or until the fillets turn white.

When the fish is cooked, remove the cover and place the fillets on warmed individual plates or a serving platter. Pour the liquid in which the fish was cooked into a saucepan, add the grapes and bring the mixture to a boil, cooking just until the grapes begin to split. Combine the arrowroot, fructose and water and mix well. Add it to the grape sauce along with the tarragon and cook, stirring constantly, until thickened. Remove from the heat and add the white sauce and again mix thoroughly. Pour the sauce over the fish fillets and serve.

PISCES MEXICANA

2 pounds white fish fillets, preferably
  sea bass or red snapper
Juice of 3 limes
1 tablespoon corn oil
2 medium onions, thinly sliced
1 4-ounce jar pimientos
3 large tomatoes, peeled and diced
1 tablespoon chopped fresh green chili pepper
1 cup finely chopped parsley

8 large sprigs parsley for garnish

Makes 8 servings
Each serving contains approximately:
2 low-fat protein portions
1/4 fat portion
1 vegetable portion
146 calories
110 mg. sodium

Wash the fish thoroughly with cold water and pat dry. Place the fish in a glass baking dish and pour the lime juice over it. Cover and refrigerate for at least 2 hours before cooking.

    Heat the corn oil in a large skillet, add the onions and cook until clear. Chop half of the pimientos and reserve the other half for garnish. Add the chopped pimientos, tomatoes, chili and parsley to the onions. Cook, covered, until there is about 1 inch of juice in the skillet. Add the fish and cook about 5 minutes on each side, or until the fish is completely white and fork tender. Serve with the sauce spooned over the top of each serving. Cut the remaining pimientos in strips and garnish each serving with the strips and parsley sprigs.

SEVICHE

1 pound fresh white fish, cut into small cubes
1/2 cup fresh lime juice
Dash Tabasco sauce
1/2 teaspoon freshly ground black pepper
2 garlic buds, minced
1 large onion, minced
1/4 cup red wine vinegar
2 teaspoons dried oregano, crushed
1/2 cup finely chopped fresh coriander
  (cilantro) or parsley
2 ripe tomatoes, finely chopped

1 4-ounce can jalapeño chili peppers, seeded,
  deveined and finely chopped, plus the
  juice from the can
1 2-ounce jar chopped pimientos

Makes 8 servings
Each serving contains approximately:
1-1/2 low-fat protein portions
1 vegetable portion
108 calories
62 mg. sodium

Place the cubed fish in a nonmetal dish. Combine the lime juice, Tabasco sauce, pepper and garlic. Pour the mixture over the fish, cover and refrigerate for 24 hours. Add all other ingredients and refrigerate for at least 3 more hours before serving.

PAELLA

12 large shrimp
12 clams, in the shell
1/2 cup olive oil
6 garlic buds, minced
2 frying chickens, cut into serving pieces and
    skinned
2 pounds lean pork, cubed
3 large onions, finely chopped
2 cups raw long-grain white rice
3 cups Unsalted Chicken Stock, page 34
1 cup dry white wine
1 teaspoon powdered saffron
1/2 teaspoon paprika
2 cups shelled peas (2 pounds unshelled)

2 large tomatoes, diced
1/4 cup freshly grated Parmesan cheese
1 4-ounce jar pimientos, cut into julienne
12 lemon wedges

Makes 12 servings
Each serving contains approximately:
4 low-fat protein portions
2 fat portions
1 starch portion
2 vegetable portions
430 calories
153 mg. sodium

Shell the shrimp, leaving the tails attached. Using a small sharp knife, make a shallow slit down the back of each shrimp and lift out the vein. If it does not all come out in one piece, use the point of the knife to scrape out the remaining portions. Wash out the incision well with cold water and set aside. Scrub the clams with a stiff brush until they are *very clean* and set aside. Heat 1/4 cup of the olive oil in a large heavy iron skillet and add the garlic. Add the chicken pieces and pork cubes and sauté until the chicken and pork are cooked and golden brown on all sides. Set aside. In a 14-inch paella pan or skillet, heavy casserole or roasting pan at least 3 inches deep, heat the remaining 1/4 cup olive oil. Add the onions and rice and cook, stirring, until the onion is tender and the rice is lightly browned, about 15 minutes.

Preheat the oven to 400°. While the rice and onions are cooking, bring the chicken stock to a boil and add the wine. Crush the saffron and paprika together using a mortar and pestle, and add to the chicken stock-wine mixture. Now add the stock mixture to the rice and onions, mixing thoroughly. Bring to a boil and arrange the browned chicken pieces and pork cubes on the top of the rice. Scatter the peas and tomatoes evenly over the top, then sprinkle with Parmesan cheese. Arrange the clams and shrimp on top. Set the pan on the floor of the oven and bake, uncovered, for 25 to 45 minutes, or until all of the liquid has been absorbed by the rice, the rice is tender and the clams are open. At no point after the paella is put into the oven should it be stirred. When the paella is done, remove it from the oven, cover loosely with a towel and allow to rest 5 minutes. Garnish with strips of pimiento and wedges of lemon and serve.

STUFFED TARRAGON TROUT
(a foolproof fish dish)

1 tablespoon unsalted butter or corn oil margarine	Makes 6 servings
2 tablespoons dried tarragon, crushed, or 6 tablespoons minced fresh tarragon	Each serving contains approximately: 1/2 fat portion
2 onions, very thinly sliced	2 low-fat protein portions
6 small rainbow trout, split and cleaned	3/4 vegetable portion
1/4 cup fresh lemon juice	152 calories
Freshly ground black pepper	28 mg. sodium
Fresh tarragon sprigs for garnish (optional)	

Preheat the oven to 500°. Melt the butter or margarine in a large skillet, add the tarragon and mix well. Add the onions, again mix well, and cook slowly until the onion is tender. While the onion is cooking, wash the trout thoroughly in cold water, scraping any remaining scales off the skin, and pat dry. Rub the split trout both inside and out with the lemon juice. Sprinkle pepper evenly over each one, both inside and out. Place the trout in a flat glass baking dish. Divide the cooked onion mixture evenly among them, stuffing the inside cavity of each trout with the onion mixture. Spread any remaining onion mixture over the top of the trout. Cover the dish tightly with a lid or aluminum foil and place in the center of the preheated 500° oven. Cook, timing carefully, for exactly 3 minutes, then turn the oven off. *Do not open the oven door for 20 minutes.* Now remove the trout from the oven and transfer to warmed individual plates or a serving platter. Garnish with tarragon sprigs, if desired. Serve with Portuguese Pilaf and Savory Tomatoes au Gratin.

If you wish, you may leave the trout in the oven longer than 20 minutes without overcooking it. This is why I call this recipe "a foolproof fish dish." The most frequent mistake made in fish preparation is overcooking it, and with this recipe there is no chance of that.

POACHED SALMON

Unsalted Court Bouillon, page 35
Salmon, amount desired (whole, half or
 steaks)

1 ounce (1/4 cup) contains approximately:
1 low-fat protein portion
55 calories
14 mg. sodium

If poaching a whole salmon, you will need 3 quarts court bouillon. Put the court bouillon in a fish poacher or a long roasting pan. If you are preparing salmon steaks or only half a salmon, use only 6 cups court bouillon and a large kettle.

Bring the court bouillon to a boil. Wrap a piece of cheesecloth around the salmon, tying the ends with twine and leaving them long enough so that the salmon can be easily lifted out of the court bouillon when done. Place the wrapped salmon in the boiling bouillon, and when it returns to a boil, reduce the heat and simmer until done. Salmon steaks or half a salmon should take only about 10 minutes, depending upon thickness. For a whole salmon, the cooking time will be about 30 minutes. Always be careful not to overcook the salmon or it will fall apart and be too dry.

Using the cheesecloth "tails," lift the salmon out of the liquid carefully so that you do not break it. Unwrap and place on a warmed serving platter. I like to serve the salmon with Sauce Hollandaise Sans Sel, bright green vegetables arranged on the platter around the salmon, and Dill Bread. To finish off this spectacular meal with an equally impressive dessert, serve Cold Orange Soufflé.

SALMON QUENELLES IN DILL SAUCE

1 cup Unsalted Chicken Stock, page 34
4 tablespoons unsalted butter or corn oil
 margarine
1/8 teaspoon white pepper
1 cup white pastry flour
2 eggs
2 egg whites
2 cups puréed salmon
Unsalted Chicken Stock for cooking
 (optional)

1-1/2 cups Dill Sauce, page 53
Dill or parsley sprigs for garnish

Makes 16 quenelles
2 contain approximately:
1-1/2 low-fat protein portions
3/4 starch portion
3-3/4 fat portions
305 calories
61 mg. sodium

Combine chicken stock and butter or margarine in a heavy saucepan. Bring to a boil and simmer until the butter or margarine is melted. Remove from the heat and add the pepper and the flour all at once, stirring vigorously with a wooden spoon. Put the mixture back on the heat and beat until it forms a ball. This will only take a couple of minutes. Remove from the heat and make a hole in the middle of the ball of dough. Break an egg into the hole, and mix the dough and egg to re-form a ball of dough. Repeat with the second egg, then the 2 egg whites, and then the 2 cups of puréed salmon. Wrap the resulting ball of dough mixture tightly in aluminum foil or waxed paper, and refrigerate until cold. Wet your hands and form the cold dough into 16 egg-shaped forms or quenelles. Place the quenelles in chicken stock or water to cover and cook, uncovered, for approximately 20 minutes. (The quenelles will be more flavorful if cooked in stock.)

When the quenelles are done they will have increased in size and will roll over easily when lifted with a spoon. Remove them from the water with a slotted spoon, draining them well before placing on plates or a serving platter. Spoon the Dill Sauce over the quenelles and garnish with dill or parlsey sprigs.

Note If you wish to cook the quenelles ahead of time, simply cook them as directed, cool to room temperature, cover and refrigerate. To reheat them, place, covered, in a preheated 350° oven for approximately 20 minutes.

FISH KEBOBS

12 small boiling onions	Makes 6 servings
1-1/2 pounds firm white fish, cut into 1-inch cubes	Each serving contains approximately:
1 green bell pepper, seeded and cut into 1-inch squares	2 low-fat protein portions
12 cherry tomatoes	1-1/2 vegetable portions
1 cup Oriental Sesame Seed Sauce, page 53	2-1/2 fat portions
	261 calories
	119 mg. sodium

Peel the onions and put them in a saucepan with water to cover. Bring to a boil, cover, reduce heat to simmer and boil for 5 minutes. Drain and set aside to cool to room temperature. Arrange the cubes of fish on long skewers, alternating with the parboiled onions, green pepper squares and cherry tomatoes. Place the skewers in a long glass baking dish and pour the Oriental Sesame Seed Sauce over them. Cover and refrigerate for at least 4 hours before barbecuing. (I prefer to marinate them for at least 24 hours, when time permits.) Broil the kebobs in the oven or barbecue over a charcoal fire until the fish is cooked, about 4 to 5 minutes on each side.

poultry

Chicken and the white meat of turkey follow fish closely as good sources of protein that are low in fat and lower than many other protein sources in sodium. In this section you will find a variety of international recipes for poultry of all types.

GAME HENS ORANGERIE

4 Cornish game hens, cut in half
Corn oil
White pepper
2 large onions, quartered
1 6-ounce can frozen unsweetened orange
   juice concentrate, thawed
2 cups dry white wine

Each serving contains approximately:
2 low-fat protein portions
1/2 fruit portion
1/2 vegetable portion
143 calories
59 mg. sodium

Preheat the oven to 350°. Lightly rub the game hen halves with corn oil and sprinkle all sides lightly with white pepper. In a shallow baking dish or roasting pan, place the halves, cut side down, each resting on an onion quarter. Place in the preheated 350° oven for 15 minutes.

While the game hens are cooking, combine the orange juice concentrate and white wine and mix thoroughly. Pour the mixture over the top of the game hens and continue to cook for 45 more minutes, basting frequently. Remove from the oven and place the game hen halves and onion quarters on warmed individual plates or a serving platter. Spoon the sauce from the baking dish over the top of each serving.

You can cook the game hens ahead of time and reheat them just before serving in a preheated 400° oven until a golden brown. I routinely prepare my game hens in this manner because they are prettier, crisper and tastier. I like to serve them with Wild Rice à l'Orange and Zucchini in Basil Butter.

ROAST CHICKEN

1 large onion, cut into quarters
1 roasting chicken
1 teaspoon corn oil
White pepper
Garlic powder

1 ounce (1 slice 3 by 2 by 1/8 inch or 1/4 cup
  chopped, without skin) contains
  approximately:
1 low-fat protein portion
55 calories
22 mg. sodium

Preheat the oven to 350°. Place the onion quarters in the cavity of the chicken. Rub the chicken with corn oil and sprinkle lightly all over with white pepper and garlic powder. Put the chicken, breast side down, in a roasting pan. Roast in the preheated 350° oven for about 1 hour or until the liquid runs clear when the chicken is tilted. Let rest for a few minutes before carving.

Note If you are going to use the chicken for salad, allow it to cool until it can be easily handled, then remove the skin and cut the meat from the bones. Refrigerate the chicken before cutting it into smaller pieces. It is easier to cut into uniform-sized cubes when cold. One 3-pound chicken yields about 3 cups chopped cooked chicken meat without skin.

CHICKEN CURAÇAO

2 tablespoons unsalted butter or corn oil
  margarine
2 teaspoons onion powder
3 whole chicken breasts, boned, skinned and
  halved
2 cups fresh orange juice
2 teaspoons freshly grated orange peel
1/4 teaspoon freshly ground black pepper
1 tablespoon grated ginger root
1 teaspoon garlic powder
1/4 cup Curaçao
1 tablespoon cornstarch

1 tablespoon cold water
2 medium oranges, peeled and sliced, for
  garnish

Makes 6 servings
Each serving contains approximately:
2 low-fat protein portions
1 fat portion
1-1/2 fruit portions
215 calories
42 mg. sodium

Preheat the oven to 350°. Melt the butter or margarine in a large skillet. Add the onion powder and mix thoroughly. Sauté the chicken breasts until a golden brown on both sides, then transfer to a baking dish. Combine the orange juice, orange peel, pepper, ginger and garlic powder and pour over the top of the chicken. Cover with a lid or aluminum foil and bake in the preheated 350° oven for 20 minutes. Remove from the oven and pour the Curaçao evenly over the top of the chicken. Re-cover and return to the oven for 20 more minutes. When the chicken is cooked, place the chicken breasts on a warmed serving platter and cover to keep warm. Place the liquid from the baking dish in a saucepan over medium heat. Combine the cornstarch and water, mix until smooth and add to the saucepan, stirring in well. Bring the mixture to a boil, reduce heat and simmer, stirring constantly, until thickened. Pour over the chicken on the serving platter and garnish with fresh orange slices.

CHICKEN CONCORD

1 cup unsweetened Concord grape juice
1 tablespoon cornstarch
1/2 teaspoon fennel seeds, lightly crushed
1 tablespoon corn oil
2 large onions, thinly sliced
3 whole chicken breasts, boned, skinned and
   halved
6 small bunches Concord grapes for garnish
   (optional)

Makes 6 servings
Each serving contains approximately:
2 low-fat protein portions
3/4 vegetable portion
3/4 fruit portion
1/2 fat portion
182 calories
45 mg. sodium

Combine the grape juice and cornstarch and mix until the cornstarch is thoroughly dissolved. Add the fennel seeds and mix well. Place the pan on low heat and slowly bring to a boil. Allow to simmer, stirring constantly with a wire whisk, until slightly thickened. Remove from the heat and set aside.

Preheat the oven to 350°. Heat the corn oil in a large skillet. Add the onions and cook until soft. Add the chicken breasts and cook until fork tender and lightly browned. Arrange the chicken breasts and onion slices in a baking dish and pour the Concord grape sauce over them. Cover with a lid or aluminum foil and place in the preheated 350° oven for 20 minutes. Garnish each serving with a small bunch of fresh Concord grapes, if available. (If unavailable, use any other grape or fresh parsley for garnish.) Serve with pilaf and a fresh green vegetable.

CHICKEN EGGS FOO YUNG

Sauce
1/4 cup sherry
1 tablespoon cornstarch
1 tablespoon cider vinegar
1/4 teaspoon garlic powder
1/8 teaspoon ground ginger
1 teaspoon fructose
1/2 cup Unsalted Beef Stock, page 33

1 cup finely chopped cooked chicken
1 cup bean sprouts, cooked and drained
1/2 cup minced green onion tops

6 eggs, lightly beaten
1 teaspoon corn oil
1/2 cup chopped green onion tops for
  garnish

Makes 4 servings
Each serving contains approximately:
1-1/2 medium-fat protein portions
1 low-fat protein portion
3/4 vegetable portion
187 calories
107 mg. sodium

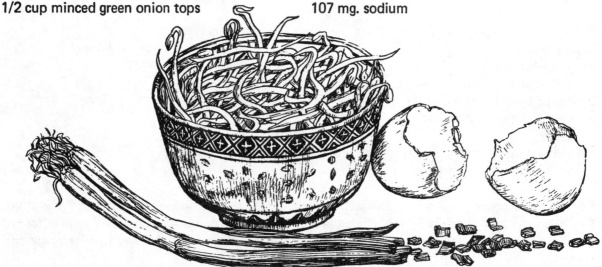

Put the sherry, cornstarch, vinegar, garlic powder, ginger and fructose in a saucepan and stir until the cornstarch is completely dissolved. Add the beef stock and cook over low heat, stirring constantly, until thickened. Set aside.

Combine the chicken, bean sprouts, minced onion tops and eggs and mix well. Heat the corn oil in a heavy iron skillet. Wipe the bottom of the skillet with a paper towel to spread the oil evenly over the entire inner surface. When the skillet is hot, pour in the egg mixture (as if making pancakes), using about 1/4 cup to form each patty. Lightly brown each patty on both sides. Continue cooking until the egg is completely set, about 5 minutes. Spoon a little of the sauce over each patty before serving, then garnish each serving with chopped green onion tops.

CHICKEN PAPRIKA

2 tablespoons unsalted butter or corn oil margarine
3 onions, finely chopped
3 garlic buds, minced
1 tablespoon paprika
2 tomatoes, peeled and diced
1 frying chicken, cut into serving pieces and skinned
1/2 cup sherry

1/2 cup sour cream

Makes 6 servings
Each serving contains approximately:
2 low-fat protein portions
1-3/4 fat portions
1-1/4 vegetable portions
221 calories
65 mg. sodium

Melt the butter or margarine in a large heavy iron skillet. Add the onions and garlic and cook over very low heat, stirring frequently, for about 30 minutes. Add the paprika and cook, stirring constantly, for another 15 minutes. Add the tomatoes, chicken pieces and sherry to the onion mixture. Bring to a boil, reduce heat, cover and simmer for about 1 hour or until the chicken is tender.

Just before serving, remove the chicken pieces and put them on warmed individual plates or a serving platter. Add the sour cream to the sauce in the pan and mix well, cooking just long enough to heat the sour cream. Spoon the sauce over the chicken. This dish is excellent with buttered noodles and Caraway Cabbage.

SMOKED TURKEY BREAST

1 tablespoon corn oil
1 tablespoon liquid smoke
1/2 teaspoon garlic powder
1/2 teaspoon ground ginger
1/8 teaspoon white pepper
1 turkey breast

1 ounce (1 slice 3 by 2 by 1/8 inch or 1/4 cup chopped, without skin) contains approximately:
1 low-fat protein portion
55 calories
23 mg. sodium

Preheat the oven to 325°. Combine the corn oil, liquid smoke, garlic powder, ginger and white pepper and mix well. Rub the mixture into the turkey breast and place it in a roasting pan, skin side up. Cook in the preheated 325° oven for 20 minutes per pound. Remove from the oven, place on a serving platter and remove the skin. Pour any liquid in the pan over the breast before serving.

Smoked Turkey Breast is good served either hot or cold, and is excellent for making sandwiches and salads.

ROAST TURKEY

3 onions, cut into quarters
1 turkey
1 tablespoon corn oil
White pepper
Garlic powder

1 ounce (1 slice 3 by 2 by 1/8 inch or 1/4 cup
    chopped, without skin) contains
    approximately:

White meat
1 low-fat protein portion
55 calories
23 mg. sodium

Dark meat
1 low-fat protein portion
55 calories
28 mg. sodium

Preheat the oven to 325°. Place the onion quarters in the cavity of the turkey. Rub the turkey with the corn oil and sprinkle it lightly all over with white pepper and garlic powder. Put the turkey, breast side down, on a rack in a flat roasting pan. (If you do not have a rack, place the turkey in the bottom of the pan.) Roast in the preheated 325° oven 20 minutes per pound.

    Remove from the oven and allow to cool slightly before placing on a serving platter. Pour the drippings in a bowl and place in the freezer. When the fat has solidified on the top (in about 30 minutes), scrape it off and discard it. Use the defatted drippings to make gravy for your turkey dinner, or store the drippings in the refrigerator to use later in stock or soup.

TURKEY CANNELLONI

1 quart low-sodium low-fat milk
2 tablespoons unsalted butter or corn oil
   margarine
1/3 cup all-purpose flour
3/4 teaspoon white pepper
1/4 teaspoon ground nutmeg
2 teaspoons olive oil
1 medium onion, minced
1/4 cup minced parsley
2 tablespoons chopped carrot
2 cups finely chopped cooked turkey
1/2 teaspoon dried oregano, crushed
1/2 teaspoon dried basil, crushed
3/4 cup dry white wine

8 Crêpes, page 148, warmed
1/4 cup Unsalted Tomato Sauce, page 47
Additional 1/4 cup low-sodium low-fat milk
1/4 cup freshly grated Parmesan cheese

Makes 8 servings
Each serving contains approximately:
1 starch portion
1/2 vegetable portion
1 low-fat protein portion
1 fat portion
1/2 low-fat milk portion
246 calories
77 mg. sodium

Put the quart of milk in a saucepan on low heat and bring just to the boiling point. In another saucepan melt the butter or margarine, add the flour, and cook, stirring constantly, for 3 minutes. *Do not brown.* Remove from the heat and add the hot milk all at once, stirring constantly with a wire whisk. Put the saucepan on low heat and cook for 20 minutes, stirring occasionally. Add 1/4 teaspoon of the white pepper and the nutmeg to the sauce. Mix well and set aside.

Heat the olive oil in a large skillet. Add the onion, parlsey and carrot. Sauté for 15 minutes or until the vegetables are tender. Add the turkey, oregano, basil, remaining 1/2 teaspoon white pepper and wine. Simmer until the wine is reduced by half. Remove from the heat and add 1-1/2 cups of the reserved white sauce to the turkey mixture and mix well.

Preheat the oven to 425°. Divide the turkey mixture equally onto the crêpes and roll them up around the filling. Place the crêpes, seam side down, in a flat baking dish. Combine the remaining 1-1/2 cups white sauce with the tomato sauce and additional 1/4 cup milk. Mix well and pour evenly over the cannelloni. Sprinkle the Parmesan cheese evenly over the top. Bake in the preheated 425° oven for 10 to 12 minutes or until the tops are lightly browned.

LITHUANIAN RABBIT

3 tablespoons unsalted butter or corn oil
   margarine
3 garlic buds, minced
1/4 teaspoon freshly ground black pepper
1 young rabbit, cut into serving pieces
1 lemon, cut in half
3 large onions, quartered
2 cups sliced fresh mushrooms (1/2 pound)
2 cups Unsalted Light Brown Sauce, page 50

Makes 6 servings
Each serving contains approximately:
3 low-fat protein portions
1-1/2 fat portions
1 vegetable portion
258 calories
72 mg. sodium

Preheat the oven to 350°. Melt the butter or margarine in a large heavy iron skillet. Add the garlic and pepper and cook for a few minutes. Rub the rabbit pieces with the lemon, add them to the skillet and brown thoroughly.

While the rabbit is browning, steam the onions over rapidly boiling water until they are fork tender and set aside. When the rabbit is brown, add the mushrooms to the skillet and continue cooking until the mushrooms are tender. Transfer the rabbit and mushrooms to a shallow baking dish and add the onions. Pour the Unsalted Light Brown Sauce over the entire dish and bake, uncovered, in the preheated 350° oven for 1 hour.

This dish may be prepared ahead of time to the point where it goes into the oven, then covered and refrigerated. Let the dish come to room temperature before putting it in the oven.

meat

Because red meats contain greater amounts of animal fat than either fish or poultry, they are usually limited in low-calorie diets. Veal is in a category by itself because it is lower in fat than other meats and it is slightly lower in sodium content. There are also meats that should be avoided completely on a sodium-restricted diet, such as ham, sausage, bacon, corned beef, frankfurters and cold cuts of all types, because of the added salt in their preparation. To replace this whole range of meats, I have included a recipe in this section for a low-sodium sausage and have created sauces (in the sauce chapter) that add the flavors associated with restricted meats to those meats allowed on your diet program.

When a recipe says to brown the meat, I mean to a very dark brown; this heavy browning greatly enhances the flavor. When marinating meats in low-sodium marinades, marinate them at least twice as long as you would when using marinades containing either salt or soy sauce. Remember that meat tenderizers, monosodium glutamate, seasoned salts, soy sauce, commercially prepared terayaki and barbecue sauces, and some of the pepper mixes such as lemon and herb peppers should be avoided on a low-sodium diet. When using herbs and spices in the absence of salt, it is actually sometimes necessary to triple the amounts called for in recipes containing salt, so do not be alarmed by what may appear to be overseasoning.

OSSO BUCO

4 slices veal shank (about 2 pounds)
1 cup dry red wine
1 16-ounce can unsalted tomatoes, mashed,
    with juice
3 onions, coarsely chopped
3 garlic buds, minced
2 bay leaves
2 teaspoons dried basil, crushed
1 teaspoon dried oregano, crushed
1/2 teaspoon freshly ground black pepper

1/4 cup finely chopped parsley
2 teaspoons freshly grated lemon peel

Makes 4 servings
Each serving contains approximately:
3 medium-fat protein portions
2-1/2 vegetable portions
288 calories
111 mg. sodium

Remove all visible fat from the veal shanks. Combine the veal shanks and 1/4 cup of the red wine in a heavy Dutch oven or soup kettle. Cover and cook for 10 minutes. Uncover and cook until all the liquid evaporates and the meat is very brown. Add the remaining 3/4 cup of wine, the mashed tomatoes and all their juice, onions, garlic, bay leaves, basil, oregano and pepper. Cover and simmer for about 2 hours, or until meat is very tender. Uncover and continue cooking until the sauce is very thick. Remove the veal shanks to individual plates and spoon the sauce evenly over each serving. Sprinkle 1 tablespoon parsley and 1/2 teaspoon lemon peel over each serving.

VEAL OSCAR

18 asparagus spears
1 tablespoon unsalted butter or corn oil
  margarine
White pepper
1-1/2 pounds veal cutlets (6 small cutlets)
1/4 pound cooked crab legs
3/4 cup Sauce Béarnaise Sans Sel, page 51

Makes 6 servings
Each serving contains approximately:
4 low-fat protein portions
2 fat portions
1/2 vegetable portion
323 calories
152 mg. sodium

Break the tough end off of each asparagus stalk by holding it in both hands and gently bending the tough end until it breaks. Steam the asparagus tips over rapidly boiling water for 3 to 5 minutes, or until crisp tender. Remove from the heat and immediately place under cold running water to stop the cooking and to preserve the color. Drain thoroughly and set aside.

    Melt the butter or margarine in a large skillet. Lightly sprinkle each veal cutlet with white pepper, place in the skillet and brown over medium heat. Continue cooking until the cutlets are fork tender, then remove from the skillet and place on a cookie sheet. Evenly divide the small amount of crab legs on each of the veal cutlets. (This is not as much crab as you would normally expect to find in a classic Veal Oscar, because crab is high in sodium. The classic combination is maintained, though, and few of your guests will realize the amount of crab is smaller than usual.) Place 3 asparagus tips on top of each serving. Spoon 2 tablespoons of the Sauce Béarnaise Sans Sel over them. Place under the broiler until the sauce is lightly browned.

STEAK AU POIVRE

1 3-pound top sirloin steak, 1-1/4 inches
  thick
2 tablespoons black peppercorns
4 teaspoons unsalted butter or corn oil
  margarine
1/2 cup dry white wine
1 tablespoon brandy

1 slice 1 by 3 by 1/4 inch contains
  approximately:
1/2 fat portion
1 low-fat protein portion
78 calories
17 mg. sodium

Prepare the steak 2 hours before serving. Remove all visible fat, wipe the steak with a damp cloth and carefully dry it. Crush the peppercorns in a mortar with a pestle or put them in a cloth and pound them with a hammer. (This amount makes a very hot pepper steak, so if you prefer a mild flavor, use less.) First, press the crushed peppercorns firmly into both sides of the steak with your hand, then smack the steak all over with the flat side of a meat cleaver to press the pepper in more securely. Cover the steak and allow it to stand for at least 2 hours at room temperature or until you are ready to cook it.

In a large cured iron skillet, melt 1 teaspoon of the butter or margarine, then wipe it out with a paper towel. Get the skillet very hot, put the steak in it and cook over very high heat for 5 minutes on each side. (This timing is for rare steak. If you prefer your steak less rare, simply cook it a little longer.)

Remove the steak to a heated platter. Pour the white wine and brandy into the hot skillet and boil for 2 minutes, stirring constantly and scraping all the drippings at the bottom of the pan into the wine. Remove from the heat and add the remaining tablespoon butter or margarine. Stir well and pour into a heated sauce dish or gravy boat. Slice the steak horizontally in very thin slices. Spoon a little of the sauce over each serving.

This recipe is a classic presentation of Steak au Poivre, which traditionally is not prepared with salt and is therefore an ideal recipe to include in a low-sodium cookbook. I always cook a 3-pound steak no matter how many people I am serving, because it makes marvelous sandwiches the next day.

NEW ENGLAND BOILED DINNER

1 3-pound lean fresh beef brisket
6 garlic buds, cut in half
3 onions, chopped
3 bay leaves
1 teaspoon whole black peppercorns
3 tablespoons pickling spices
4 small carrots, scraped and halved lengthwise
4 potatoes, peeled and cut into quarters
2 small heads cabbage, cut into quarters

Makes 8 servings
Each serving contains approximately:
3 low-fat protein portions (1 slice brisket
    2 by 3 by 1/8 inch = 1 portion X the
    number you wish)
1 starch portion
1 vegetable portion
260 calories
139 mg. sodium

Put the beef brisket in a large saucepan or soup kettle and cover it with cold water. Add all remaining ingredients, except the carrots, potatoes and cabbage, and bring to a boil. Reduce the heat to low and simmer for 3 to 4 hours with the lid slightly ajar so that the steam can escape. Remove from the heat, let cool to room temperature and refrigerate overnight.

The next day, remove the fat that has solidified on top. Bring the brisket and stock mixture slowly to a boil and add the carrots and potatoes. Cook for 30 minutes, or until the vegetables are almost tender. Add the cabbage and cook for approximately 15 more minutes, or until the cabbage can easily be pierced with a fork. (Do not overcook the cabbage or it will be mushy.) Serve with Mustard Sauce and hot Swedish Rye Bread.

MARTINI POT ROAST

1 teaspoon corn oil
1/2 cup all-purpose flour
1 teaspoon white pepper
1 3-pound lean pot roast, cut of choice
   (round-bone and 7-bone cuts are good)
1-1/2 cups dry vermouth
3 cups Unsalted Beef Stock, page 33
2 tablespoons dried juniper berries
1/2 teaspoon dried basil, crushed
1/2 teaspoon dried marjoram, crushed
1/2 teaspoon dried thyme, crushed
2 bay leaves
4 small potatoes, peeled and cut in half

4 onions, cut in half
4 carrots, scraped and halved lengthwise

Makes 8 servings
Each serving contains approximately:
3 low-fat protein portions (1 slice 2 by 3 by
   1/8 inch = 1 portion X the number you
   wish)
1-1/2 vegetable portions
1 starch portion
273 calories
104 mg. sodium

Put the corn oil in a large heavy iron skillet and heat until the pan is very hot. Combine flour and white pepper in a paper bag, add the pot roast and shake until completely coated with the flour mixture. Put the floured roast in the skillet and brown over medium heat, turning frequently, for 1-1/2 hours or until a very dark, burned-looking brown. Add 1/2 cup of the vermouth and

simmer until the vermouth cooks away. Turn the pot roast over, add another 1/2 cup of vermouth and again simmer until dry. Turn the pot roast over again, add the remaining 1/2 cup of vermouth and simmer until dry. Combine the beef stock with the juniper berries, basil, marjoram, thyme and bay leaves and mix well. Pour the beef stock mixture over the pot roast, cover and simmer for about 1-1/2 hours. Add the potatoes, onions and carrots and cook until the vegetables are tender.

I call this Martini Pot Roast because it is cooked in vermouth and seasoned with juniper berries, just like gin.

ENCHILADAS HAMBURGUESA

1 tablespoon corn oil
1 onion, finely chopped
1-1/2 tablespoons chili powder
1 teaspoon ground cumin
3 medium tomatoes, peeled and diced
1/2 pound ground round, cooked
1/2 cup Unsalted Beef Stock, page 33
1-1/2 cups grated low-sodium cheddar cheese
8 corn tortillas, warmed
1 large onion, chopped (optional)

Makes 8 servings
Each serving contains approximately:
1 medium-fat protein portion
3/4 high-fat protein portion
1 starch portion
1/4 fat portion
1 vegetable portion
253 calories
46 mg. sodium

Preheat the oven to 350°. Heat the corn oil in a large skillet and add the finely chopped onion. Cook until clear and tender. Add the chili powder and cumin and mix well. Add the tomatoes, ground round and beef stock, mix well and cook for 5 minutes over low heat. Then add 3/4 cup of the grated cheese and mix thoroughly. Spoon an equal amount of the mixture evenly down the center of each tortilla. Roll the tortilla around it and place seam side down in a 7- by 12-inch baking dish. Spoon any remaining meat mixture over the enchiladas in the dish, then sprinkle the remaining 3/4 cup of cheese evenly over the top. Cover the baking dish and bake in the preheated 350° oven for 30 minutes. Sprinkle the chopped onion over the top before serving, if desired. Serve with Gazpacho as an appetizer, Portuguese Pilaf, and fresh fruit for dessert.

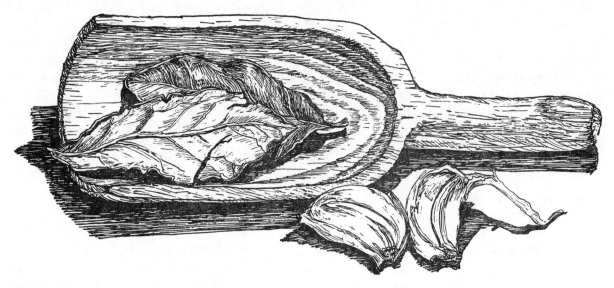

IRISH STEW

2 pounds lean lamb, cut into 1-inch cubes
1/2 cup all-purpose flour
4 teaspoons unsalted butter or corn oil
   margarine
1 onion, finely chopped
2 cups sliced fresh mushrooms (1/2 pound)
1/2 cup finely chopped parsley
2 garlic buds, minced
2 bay leaves
1 teaspoon dried thyme, crushed
1 teaspoon dried summer savory, crushed
1 teaspoon freshly ground black pepper
2 cups water

2 cups dry red wine
2 turnips, diced
16 small boiling onions
2 cups shelled peas (2 pounds unshelled)

Makes 8 servings
Each serving contains approximately:
3 low-fat protein portions
2-1/2 vegetable portions
1/2 fat portion
251 calories
111 mg. sodium

Put the cubed lamb and flour in a paper bag and shake it until the meat is thoroughly coated. Melt the butter or margarine in a large heavy pan or soup kettle. Add the chopped onion and mushrooms and sauté until tender; remove from the pan and set aside. Do not wash the pan. Add the lamb to the hot pan and brown thoroughly. When the meat is a rich, dark brown, return the onion-mushroom mixture to the pan and add the parsley, garlic, bay leaves, thyme, summer savory, pepper, 1 cup of the water and 1 cup of the wine. Simmer, covered, for 1 hour. Then add the remaining cup water and wine and simmer for 30 minutes. Add the turnips and boiling onions and continue simmering for 1 more hour. About 10 minutes before serving, add the peas and cook until they are just tender.

Though Irish stew is traditionally served with colcannon, a combination of mashed potatoes, cooked cabbage and green onions, I like to serve it on St. Patrick's Day with Irish Soda Bread and St. Patrick's Day Potato Salad instead.

INDONESIAN BARBECUED LAMB

1/2 cup unsalted peanut butter
1/4 cup fresh lemon juice
1/4 cup dry sherry
1/4 cup fructose
1 tablespoon garlic powder
1/2 leg of lamb, butterflied, with all visible fat removed (about 3 pounds)

1 ounce (1 slice 3 by 2 by 1/8 inch or 1/4 cup chopped) contains approximately:

1 low-fat protein portion
55 calories
20 mg. sodium

Makes about 1 cup marinade/sauce
1 tablespoon contains approximately:
1/2 fruit portion
1/4 high-fat protein portion
44 calories
2 mg. sodium

Combine all ingredients, except the lamb, and mix well. Place the lamb in a container just large enough to hold the meat so that the marinade covers it. Pour the marinade over the lamb, cover and refrigerate for at least 24 hours before barbecuing. Turn the meat in the marinade every few hours so that as much of the marinade as possible is absorbed.

Though this lamb is best cooked over charcoal, it can be broiled. The cooking time depends on how you like it served. At 12 to 15 minutes per side, the lamb will be medium rare. Increase this time according to your taste. Reserve the marinade to serve as a sauce with the lamb.

I got the idea for this recipe at Trader Vic's in San Francisco. I ordered Indonesian lamb there, and it came with a peanut butter sauce on the side. I simply adapted the idea and made the sauce a marinade as well.

Variation Substitute lamb chops for the leg of lamb.

MINTED LAMB CHOPS

4 loin lamb chops, 1-1/2 inches thick
1 lemon, cut in half
Onion powder
1/4 cup Unsalted Mayonnaise, page 52
1 slice low-sodium bread, crumbled
2 tablespoons fructose
1 cup finely chopped fresh mint

Makes 4 servings
Each serving contains approximately:
3 low-fat protein portions
1/4 starch portion
2 fat portions
1/2 fruit portion
293 calories
65 mg. sodium

Preheat the oven to 500°. Remove all visible fat from the lamb chops and place them in a shallow baking dish. Rub both sides of each chop with lemon, then sprinkle both sides with onion powder. Combine the mayonnaise, bread crumbs, fructose and mint and mix well. Cover each lamb chop with the mint mixture, pressing it down firmly with your hands. Put the lamb chops

in the preheated 500° oven for 4 minutes. *Then turn the oven off and do not open the door for 30 minutes.* After 30 minutes has passed, remove from the oven and serve.

These marvelous-tasting lamb chops are special because they can be prepared ahead of time. It will appear to your guests that only a magician could prepare the chops and be only 34 minutes from serving this elegant entrée.

Anyone who likes mint jelly served with lamb will love this recipe. Even those who don't may still like it, because the fresh mint gives a more subtle flavor to the lamb than the jelly.

Variation This same recipe works equally well for a rack of lamb. When cooking a rack, place it rib side down and pack the mint mixture on top.

INDIAN LAMB CURRY

3 tablespoons unsalted butter or corn oil margarine
3 onions, minced
5 tablespoons all-purpose flour
2 tablespoons curry powder
1/2 teaspoon ground ginger
2 cups Unsalted Chicken Stock, page 34, heated
2 cups low-sodium low-fat milk, heated
6 cups cubed cooked lamb, with all visible fat removed

1 tablespoon fresh lemon juice

Makes 8 servings
Each serving contains approximately:
3 low-fat protein portions
1 fat portion
3/4 vegetable portion
1/4 starch portion
1/4 low-fat milk portion
278 calories
73 mg. sodium

Melt the butter or margarine in a large saucepan or soup kettle. Add the minced onion and cook until the onion is clear and tender. Combine the flour, curry powder and ginger and add to the onion, stirring constantly until a thick paste is formed. Add the hot chicken stock and stir until it again becomes a thick paste. Slowly add the hot milk, stirring constantly. Continue to cook over low heat, stirring occasionally, until the sauce has thickened slightly, about 45 minutes. Add the cooked lamb and lemon juice. Heat thoroughly and serve over plain cooked rice.

When serving curry, have a large selection of condiments, such as Major Jones Chutney, raisins, chopped unsalted peanuts, minced parsley and chopped hard-cooked eggs. For people who do not wish to add calories with the condiments, try grated fresh orange or lemon peel. It is colorful, delicious and almost calorie free.

LOW-SODIUM SAUSAGE

2 pounds lean pork, all visible fat removed,
   ground twice
1 tablespoon dried sage, crushed
1 teaspoon garlic powder
1 teaspoon onion powder
1 teaspoon ground mace
1 teaspoon freshly ground black pepper
1/4 teaspoon ground allspice

1/4 teaspoon ground cloves

Makes 12 patties
Each patty contains approximately:
2 medium-fat protein portions
150 calories
48 mg. sodium

Combine all ingredients in a large mixing bowl, mix thoroughly and form into 12 patties.

    I like to make these ahead and freeze them in individual plastic bags. Then whenever you want sausage it's handy. I have found that everyone seems to like my low-sodium sausage better than the high-sodium greasy variety available in the market. If you have missed sausage for breakfast on your low-sodium diet, your problems are over.

CANTONESE SWEET AND SOUR PORK

1 20-ounce can pineapple chunks
   in natural juice, undrained
2 tablespoons cornstarch
1/3 cup cider vinegar
1/4 cup fructose
2 teaspoons grated ginger root
Dash cayenne pepper
1 tablespoon fresh lemon juice
4 cups cubed cooked pork roast (1-inch
   cubes), with all visible fat removed
1 cup sliced fresh mushrooms (1/4 pound)
1 green bell pepper, seeded and thinly sliced

1 medium onion, thinly sliced
1 6-ounce can water chestnuts, thinly sliced
4 cups cooked long-grain white rice, hot

Makes 8 servings
Each serving contains approximately:
2 medium-fat protein portions
1 fruit portion
1/2 vegetable portion
1 starch portion
273 calories
49 mg. sodium

Drain the juice from the pineapple chunks and pour it into a large saucepan. Set the pineapple chunks aside to add later. Add the cornstarch to the juice and stir until the cornstarch is thoroughly dissolved. Add the cider vinegar, fructose and grated ginger root and cook, stirring constantly, over medium heat until the sauce has thickened. Remove from the heat and add the cayenne pepper, lemon juice, pineapple and pork. Mix well and allow to stand for 1 hour. Add the mushrooms, bell pepper, onion and water chestnuts and cook over medium heat until the vegetables are just crisp tender. Spoon each serving over 1/2 cup of the cooked white rice.

ITALIAN LIVER

1 teaspoon dried oregano, crushed
1/4 teaspoon freshly ground black pepper
1 cup dry red wine
1 pound calves' liver, thinly sliced
1 tablespoon corn oil
4 medium onions, thinly sliced

Makes 6 servings
Each serving contains approximately:
2-1/2 medium-fat protein portions
1-1/2 vegetable portions
226 calories
171 mg. sodium

Combine the oregano, pepper and red wine and mix thoroughly. Marinate the liver in the mixture for at least 2 hours.

Heat the corn oil in a large skillet. Add the onions and sauté until a golden brown in color. Remove the liver from the marinade and place it in the pan with the onions. Cook to desired doneness. Remember, cooking it too long tends to toughen it. Remove the liver and onions to individual plates or a serving platter and serve immediately.

breads, pancakes and cereals

When I first started working on *Secrets of Salt-Free Cooking,* I realized how many commonplace products such as graham crackers and English muffins are not available in the market without added salt. For this reason I have included recipes for these basic items. I also found that recipes requiring salt, soda, baking powder and other high-sodium ingredients cannot be altered for a low-sodium diet simply by eliminating the things high in sodium. Because of this, I have added ingredients not usually found in many bread and similar recipes to improve the flavor and eliminate the "flat" taste often associated with low-sodium bread products.

Some of these ingredients, such as vinegar, lemon juice, Tabasco sauce, cayenne pepper and the full range of herbs and spices, are available in the market. Other ingredients, such as low-sodium baking powder, potassium bicarbonate, low-sodium milk and Bakon Yeast, usually have to be purchased either in a health food store or at a pharmacy. If you are unable to find low-sodium baking powder you can have your own pharmacist make it for you. I have included its formula in Secret Suggestions and Important Facts on page 177. In that section you will also find directions for using these ingredients.

All of the recipes in this section have been tested with both low-sodium milk, as listed in each recipe, and regular non-fat milk, and they work equally well with both. The recipes all call for low-sodium milk because it is possible to save many milligrams of sodium per day by using nothing but low-sodium milk both for drinking and cooking. Its use is a good habit for anyone on a salt-restricted diet to acquire.

One additional note on ingredients: Always check the expiration date on yeast packages. It is important to the success of your breads that the yeast you use not be too old, or the bread will not rise.

LOW-SODIUM WHITE BREAD

1 cup low-sodium low-fat milk, heated to
   lukewarm (110° to 115°)
1 tablespoon fresh lemon juice
2 packages (2 tablespoons) active dry yeast
   (check date on package)
2 tablespoons fructose
1 egg, lightly beaten, or
   1/2 cup liquid egg substitute
1/4 cup corn oil

3-1/4 cups all-purpose flour
Unsalted butter or corn oil margarine,
   softened, for glazing (optional)

Makes 1 loaf; 20 slices
1 slice contains approximately:
1-1/2 starch portions
105 calories
5 mg. sodium

Combine the milk and lemon juice and mix well. Add the yeast and fructose and again mix well. Set aside out of a draft and allow to double in bulk. This takes only a few minutes. Combine the egg or egg substitute and corn oil and mix well. Add the yeast mixture to the egg-oil mixture, again mixing well. Add the flour, a little at a time, until thoroughly mixed. You will have to knead the last 1/2 cup of flour in with your hands. Cover with a tea towel and allow to rise in a warm place until double in bulk, about 1-1/2 hours. Then punch down and knead on a floured board for 10 minutes, or until the dough is smooth and elastic. Lightly rub the dough ball with butter or margarine, cover with a tea towel and allow to rise again until double in bulk, about 30 minutes. Knead the dough again briefly and form it into a loaf shape. Place the dough in a greased 9- by 5- by 3-inch loaf pan, cover with a tea towel and allow to rise until nearly double in bulk, about 30 minutes.

While the bread is rising the third time, preheat the oven to 375°. Bake for 40 minutes or until it is a golden brown and sounds hollow when tapped. If you want to glaze the bread, rub the top of the loaf with a little butter or margarine 3 or 4 minutes before the baking time is completed. Remove the bread from the oven, place it on its side for 5 minutes, then turn out on a rack and cool to room temperature. The loaf is much easier to slice when it is cool. If you wish to serve the bread hot, slice it, butter it if desired, wrap it in foil and reheat in the oven.

Low-Sodium Whole Wheat Bread Variation Substitute whole wheat flour for the all-purpose flour and proceed as directed.

Crunchy Low-Sodium Wheatberry Bread Variation Substitute whole wheat flour for the all-purpose flour. Soak 1/4 cup wheatberries in water to cover for at least 24 hours, drain and add with the yeast and fructose to the milk-lemon juice mixture. Proceed as directed.

FRENCH BREAD

1/2 cup low-sodium low-fat milk, at the
   boiling point
1 cup boiling water
1 envelope (1 tablespoon) active dry yeast
   (check date on package)
1/4 cup lukewarm water (110° to 115°)
4 teaspoons unsalted butter or margarine,
   melted
2 tablespoons fructose
4 cups unbleached white four, sifted

2 tablespoons cornmeal
1 egg white, beaten
1 tablespoon cold water

Makes 2 long loaves; each loaf makes
   20 slices
1 slice contains approximately:
3/4 starch portion
53 calories
2 mg. sodium

Combine the hot milk and boiling water. Mix well and set aside to cool slightly. Add the yeast to the lukewarm water and set aside out of a draft to double in bulk. This takes only a few minutes. Combine the yeast with the milk-water mixture, then add the butter or margarine and 1 tablespoon of the fructose and mix well.

In a large mixing bowl, combine the remaining 1 tablespoon fructose and the flour and mix well. Make a well in the center of the dry ingredients and pour the liquid ingredients into it. Mix thoroughly but do not knead. Cover with a lightly dampened tea towel and set in a warm place to rise until double in bulk, about 2 hours. Push the dough down with your hands and place on a floured board. Divide it into 2 equal portions and form each portion into a long, oblong shape. Roll one long edge of the oblong to the center. Repeat with the second long edge, so the two rolls meet in the center. Taper the ends of each loaf slightly with your hands. (The purpose of rolling the dough instead of just forming into loaves is so that the loaves will be rounded rather than flat.) Lightly sprinkle the bottom of a cookie sheet with the cornmeal and place the 2 loaves, seam side down, on the sheet. Using sharp, pointed scissors, cut 1/4 inch diagonal slits across the top of each loaf about 3 inches apart. (It is important to do this with scissors instead of a knife, because a knife will mash the dough flat.) Set the loaves in a warm place to rise until not quite double in bulk.

Preheat the oven to 400°. Place a pan filled with boiling water to 1 inch on the bottom of the oven. Place the loaves on a center rack and bake for 15 minutes in the preheated 400° oven. Reduce the temperature to 350° and continue baking for 30 minutes longer. Just before removing the bread from the oven, combine the egg white and cold water and mix well. Brush the top of each loaf with the glazing mixture and continue baking 4 to 5 minutes.

Recipes for French bread are rarely found in cookbooks. It is something people always buy in bakeries. French bread from bakeries, however, contains salt and therefore is not suitable for a low-sodium diet. You will find French bread is easy to make because it requires no kneading.

IRISH SODA BREAD OR BLARNEY BREAD
(because it's a fake)

2 cups all-purpose flour
1 tablespoon low-sodium baking powder
1/2 teaspoon potassium bicarbonate
4 teaspoons fructose
4 tablespoons unsalted butter or corn oil
  margarine, chilled
2/3 cup low-sodium low-fat milk
1 teaspoon fresh lemon juice
1 egg, lightly beaten
1/2 cup raisins

2 teaspoons caraway seeds
Low-sodium milk for glazing

Makes 1 loaf; 20 slices
1 slice contains approximately:
1 starch portion
1/4 fruit portion
80 calories
6 mg. sodium

Preheat the oven to 325°. Combine the flour, baking powder, potassium bicarbonate and fructose in a large mixing bowl and mix well. Add the butter or margarine and, using a pastry blender, blend the mixture until it is the consistency of coarse cornmeal; set aside. Mix together the milk and lemon juice, combine with the egg and mix again. Then add the liquid ingredients to the butter-flour mixture and mix well. Mix in the raisins and caraway seeds. Remove the dough to a

floured board and knead for 2 or 3 minutes or until smooth and elastic. Place the dough in a greased and floured 8-inch round pan and press it down so that the dough fills the entire pan. Cut a deep crease in the top of the bread so the sides will not crack while the bread is baking. Brush the top lightly with milk and bake in the preheated 375° oven for 35 to 40 minutes, or until a light golden brown. Remove from the oven and let cool 5 minutes, then turn out of the pan, place on a rack and cool to room temperature. The loaf is much easier to slice when cool. If you wish to serve the bread hot, slice it, butter it if desired, wrap it in foil and reheat in the oven.

Next St. Patrick's Day, fool your Irish friends with low-sodium Blarney Bread and tell them it is Irish Soda Bread. Of course, the traditional recipe for soda bread is far too high in sodium to appear in a low-sodium cookbook.

ZUCCHINI BREAD

1-1/2 cups shredded zucchini	1-3/4 cups all-purpose flour
1 tablespoon fresh lemon juice	1/4 cup minced or ground walnuts
3/4 cup fructose	
1/2 cup corn oil	Makes 1 loaf; 20 slices
1 egg, at room temperature	1 slice contains approximately:
1 teaspoon vanilla extract	1-3/4 starch portions
1-1/2 teaspoons ground cinnamon	1/2 fat portion
3/4 teaspoon low-sodium baking powder	146 calories
1/4 teaspoon potassium bicarbonate	4 mg. sodium
1/4 teaspoon ground ginger	

Preheat the oven to 325°. Combine the zucchini and lemon juice and set aside. Combine the fructose, corn oil, egg and vanilla extract and mix well. Combine all remaining ingredients, except the walnuts, and mix well. Combine the fructose-oil mixture with the dry ingredients and mix until well blended, scraping the sides of the bowl frequently. Fold in the zucchini-lemon juice mixture and the walnuts. Put the dough in a greased and floured 9- by 5-inch loaf pan and bake in the center of the preheated 325° oven for approximately 1 hour and 15 minutes or until a knife inserted in the center comes out clean. Remove from the oven and let cool on its side for 5 minutes, then turn out of the pan, place on a rack and cool to room temperature.

When the bread is cool, wrap it tightly in aluminum foil or place it in a plastic bag and store in the refrigerator. To serve, slice thinly, wrap in foil and reheat in the oven. Of course, the bread can be eaten right after it is baked, but I think it tastes even better the next day.

SWEDISH RYE BREAD

1-1/2 cups lukewarm water (110° to 115°)
2 packages (2 tablespoons) active dry yeast
  (check date on packages)
3 tablespoons molasses
3 tablespoons fructose
3 tablespoons freshly grated orange peel
1 tablespoon fennel seeds
1 tablespoon caraway seeds
2-1/2 cups rye flour, sifted

2 tablespoons unsalted butter or corn oil
  margarine
2-1/2 cups all-purpose flour
Additional all-purpose flour for kneading

Makes 2 loaves; each loaf makes 20 slices
1 slice contains approximately:
3/4 starch portion
53 calories
3 mg. sodium

Combine the lukewarm water and yeast in a large mixing bowl. Set aside out of a draft and allow to double in bulk. This takes only a few minutes. Add the molasses, fructose, orange peel and fennel and caraway seeds to the yeast mixture. Slowly add the rye flour and butter or margarine and mix well. Add the all-purpose flour, a little at a time, working it in as you do. It will be necessary to knead the last of the flour into the dough on a lightly floured board. Continue kneading the dough until it is well mixed, then place it back in the bowl. Cover with a lightly dampened tea towel and allow to rise in a warm place until double in bulk, about 1-1/2 hours. Punch down the dough and knead it on a lightly floured board until it is smooth and elastic. Place the dough back in the bowl, cover with a lightly dampened tea towel and allow to again double in bulk, about 30 minutes. Punch down, knead lightly on a floured board and divide into 2 equal parts. Form each half into a loaf shape and place in greased and floured 9- by 5- by 3-inch loaf pans. Cover the pans with a lightly dampened cloth and allow to again almost double in bulk, about 30 minutes.

During the third rising, preheat the oven to 375°. Bake the loaves in the preheated 375° oven for 30 minutes, or until they are a rich brown and sound hollow when tapped. Remove the loaves from the oven, place them on their sides for 5 minutes, then turn out on a rack and cool to room temperature. The loaves are much easier to slice when they are cool. If you wish to serve the bread hot, cool it first, slice it, butter it if desired, wrap it in foil and reheat in the oven.

Variation I often put this bread dough into 12 tiny loaf pans, and serve each guest one whole tiny loaf of bread.

BANANA NUT BREAD

1/3 cup chopped walnuts
1/2 cup low-sodium low-fat milk
2 teaspoons fresh lemon juice
6 tablespoons unsalted butter or corn oil
  margarine
1/2 cup fructose
2 eggs, lightly beaten
1 teaspoon vanilla extract
2 cups unbleached white flour, sifted
4 teaspoons low-sodium baking powder

3 medium bananas, mashed (1 cup)

Makes 1 loaf; 20 slices
Each slice contains approximately:
1 fat portion
1/2 fruit portion
1 starch portion
135 calories
8 mg. sodium

Preheat the oven to 350°. Put the chopped walnuts on a cookie sheet in the preheated 350° oven for about 8 to 10 minutes, or until golden brown. Watch them carefully as they burn easily. Set aside. (Leave the oven on.)

Combine the milk and lemon juice, mix well and set aside. Cream together the butter or margarine and fructose and mix in the eggs, vanilla extract and milk-lemon juice mixture. Combine the flour and baking powder in a large mixing bowl. Slowly add the liquid ingredients, mixing thoroughly. Add the mashed bananas and toasted walnuts and mix well. Pour into a greased and floured 9- by 5- by 3-inch loaf pan and bake in the preheated 350° oven for approximately 1 hour and 15 minutes, or until a knife inserted in the center comes out clean. Remove from the oven and place on its side 5 minutes, then turn out of the pan, place on a rack and cool to room temperature. Wrap in foil or put in a sealed plastic bag and refrigerate. If possible, keep for 2 days before serving; the flavor improves.

When ready to serve, slice the bread, wrap in foil and reheat in the oven. You may wish to spread each slice lightly with unsalted butter or corn oil margarine before reheating. This bread freezes beautifully and can be made ahead in large quantities for parties. It also makes an ideal gift for a friend on a low-sodium diet.

LETTUCE BREAD

2/3 cup fructose
1/2 cup corn oil
1 egg, lightly beaten
1-1/2 cups all-purpose flour
4 teaspoons low-sodium baking powder
1/4 teaspoon potassium bicarbonate
1/4 teaspoon ground mace
1/8 teaspoon ground ginger
2 teaspoons freshly grated lemon peel
2 teaspoons fresh lemon juice

1 cup finely chopped lettuce
1/4 cup finely chopped walnuts

Makes 1 loaf; 20 slices
1 slice contains approximately:
1-1/2 starch portions
1/2 fat portion
128 calories
4 mg. sodium

Preheat the oven to 350°. Combine the fructose, corn oil and egg and mix well. Set aside. In another bowl, combine the flour, baking powder, potassium bicarbonate, mace and ginger and mix well. Combine the wet ingredients with the dry ingredients and again mix well. Add the lemon peel, lemon juice, lettuce and walnuts to the batter and mix well. Pour the batter into a greased and floured 9- by 5- by 3-inch loaf pan. Bake in the preheated 350° oven for about 1 hour or until a knife inserted in the center comes out clean. Remove from the oven and allow to cool on its side for 5 minutes, then turn out of the pan, place on a rack and cool to room temperature. To serve the bread hot, slice it, butter it if desired, wrap it in foil and reheat in the oven.

DILL BREAD

1 package (1 tablespoon) active dry yeast
  (check date on package)
1/4 cup lukewarm water (110° to 115°)
2 cups (1/2 pint) low-fat cottage cheese,
  rinsed, page 178
1 tablespoon fructose
1/4 cup minced onion
1 egg, lightly beaten
2 tablespoons dill seeds

1/8 teaspoon cayenne pepper
2 cups all-purpose flour

Makes 1 loaf; 20 slices
1 slice contains approximately:
1 starch portion
70 calories
98 mg. sodium

Add the yeast to the lukewarm water and allow to stand out of a draft until double in bulk. This takes only a few minutes. Warm the cottage cheese in a saucepan. Add the yeast mixture, fructose, onion, egg, dill seeds and cayenne pepper and mix well. Cover with a tea towel and allow to stand in a warm place for several hours, or until double in bulk.

Preheat the oven to 375°. Stir dough until again reduced to original size and put in a well-greased 9- by 5- by 3-inch loaf pan. Cover the pan and allow the dough to again double in bulk. Bake in the preheated 375° oven for 45 to 50 minutes, or until it is a golden brown. Remove from the oven and allow to cool on its side for 5 minutes, then turn out of the pan, place on a rack and cool to room temperature. If you wish to serve the bread hot, slice it, butter it if desired, wrap it in foil and reheat in the oven.

GINGERBREAD MUFFINS

2 teaspoons dry instant coffee
1/4 cup hot water
1/4 cup cold water
1-1/2 cups whole wheat pastry flour
4 teaspoons low-sodium baking powder
1/4 cup fructose
1 teaspoon ground ginger
1 teaspoon ground cinnamon
1/2 teaspoon ground cloves
1 egg yolk
1/4 teaspoon cider vinegar

1/4 cup corn oil
1/2 cup raisins
1/8 teaspoon cream of tartar
2 egg whites

Makes 12 2-1/2-inch muffins
1 muffin contains approximately:
1 starch portion
1 fruit portion
110 calories
12 mg. sodium

Preheat the oven to 400°. Lightly grease 12 2-1/2-inch muffin tins and set aside. Combine the instant coffee and hot water and mix until the coffee is thoroughly dissolved. Add the cold water, mix well and set aside. Combine the flour, baking powder, fructose, ginger, cinnamon and cloves and mix well. In another bowl, combine the egg yolk, cider vinegar, corn oil and reserved coffee and mix well. Add the liquid ingredients to the dry ingredients and stir until well mixed. Add the raisins and mix well, leaving slightly lumpy; set aside.

Add the cream of tartar to the egg whites and beat until stiff but not dry. Fold the egg whites into the batter, being careful not to overmix. Fill 12 greased 2-1/2-inch muffin tins about two-thirds full and immediately place the tins in the center of the preheated 400° oven. Bake for 25 minutes. Let cool slightly before removing from tins.

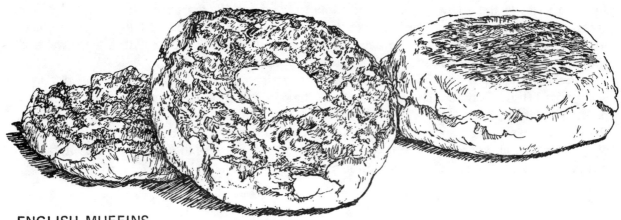

ENGLISH MUFFINS

1 cup low-sodium low-fat milk, at the
    boiling point
2 tablespoons honey
1 tablespoon fresh lemon juice
3 tablespoons unsalted butter or corn oil
    margarine
1 package (1 tablespoon) active dry yeast
    (check date on package)
1/4 cup lukewarm water (110° to 115°)
1 egg

1/8 teaspoon cream of tartar
4 cups unbleached white flour, sifted
1/2 cup cornmeal

Makes 20 muffins
1 muffin contains approximately:
2 starch portions
140 calories
6 mg. sodium

Combine the hot milk, honey, lemon juice and butter or margarine in a large mixing bowl and let
cool to lukewarm. Add the yeast to the water and allow to stand out of a draft until double in
bulk. This takes only a few minutes. Then add the yeast mixture to the milk mixture. Combine
the egg and cream of tartar in a small mixing bowl, lightly beat together with a fork or a wire
whisk and add to the milk mixture, blending well. Slowly stir in the flour, a little at a time. When
all of the flour has been added, knead the dough in the bowl until well mixed. Remove to a
floured board and knead until shiny and elastic. Wash the bowl in which you were mixing the
dough, dry thoroughly and lightly grease with unsalted butter or margarine. Return the dough
ball to the bowl and cover with a tea towel. Place in a warm spot and let rise to double in bulk,

about 1-1/2 hours. Put the dough ball on a floured board, punch down and knead again. Let the dough rest for 2 minutes.

Sprinkle 2 cookie sheets with half of the cornmeal. Roll the dough out into a large circle 1/4 inch thick and cut into 3-1/2-inch rounds using a biscuit cutter. (The lid from a wide-mouth jar will also work.) After cutting out 12 muffins, place them on the cornmeal-sprinkled cookie sheets. Then form the remaining dough back into a ball and again roll it out 1/4 inch thick, cutting as many more muffins as possible and repeating this process until you have 20 muffin rounds in all. Sprinkle the top of each muffin with a little of the remaining cornmeal and spread it evenly over the tops, using your finger tips. Cover both pans of muffins lightly with a tea towel and allow to rise in a warm place until approximately double in height.

To cook the muffins, use a griddle lightly greased with unsalted butter or margarine. Cook on medium heat approximately 8 to 10 minutes on each side. Cool muffins on a rack.

I like to split English muffins and lightly spread each half with unsalted butter or margarine, then put the muffins under a broiler until lightly browned. Also try them in the recipe for Eggs Benedict in this book.

PINEAPPLE MUFFINS

2 cups all-purpose flour
2 tablespoons low-sodium baking powder
3 tablespoons fructose
1 egg
1-1/2 teaspoons vanilla extract
1/4 cup corn oil
1 20-ounce can crushed pineapple
   in natural juice, undrained

Makes 16 muffins
Each muffin contains approximately:
1 starch portion
1 fruit portion
110 calories
6 mg. sodium

Preheat the oven to 425°. Put the flour in a large bowl. Add the baking powder and fructose and mix thoroughly. In another mixing bowl, combine the egg, vanilla extract and corn oil and beat lightly with a fork or a wire whisk. Add the crushed pineapple and all of the juice from the can to the egg mixture and mix thoroughly. Pour the wet ingredients into the dry ingredients and stir until well mixed, being careful not to overmix the batter. Fill 16 greased 2-1/2-inch muffin tins two-thirds full. Bake in the preheated 425° oven for 25 minutes. Let cool slightly before removing from tins.

WHITE CRACKERS

2 cups all-purpose flour
1/4 teaspoon garlic powder
1/4 teaspoon onion powder
5 tablespoons corn oil
1/2 cup water
2 tablespoons mustard seeds

Makes 50 crackers
2 crackers contain approximately:
1 starch portion
70 calories
Trace mg. sodium

Preheat the oven to 425°. Mix together the flour and garlic and onion powders in a large bowl. Combine the corn oil and water and mix well. Combine the dry ingredients with the wet ingredients and again mix well. Transfer the dough to a floured board and knead until it no longer sticks to your fingers. Using a rolling pin lightly dusted with flour, roll the dough out in a large square approximately 1/8 inch thick. Sprinkle the mustard seeds evenly over the square and roll the seeds lightly into the surface of the dough with the rolling pin. Cut into 2-inch squares and place the squares, well spaced, on greased or Teflon cookie sheets. Bake for 8 to 10 minutes in the preheated 425° oven. Remove from the oven and cool to room temperature before removing from the cookie sheet. Store in an airtight container.

WHOLE WHEAT CRACKERS

2 cups whole wheat flour
1/4 teaspoon garlic powder
1/4 teaspoon onion powder
Dash cayenne pepper
5 tablespoons corn oil
1/2 cup water
2 tablespoons sesame seeds

Makes 50 crackers
2 crackers contain approximately:
1 starch portion
70 calories
Trace mg. sodium

Preheat the oven to 425°. Mix together the flour, garlic powder, onion powder and cayenne pepper in a large bowl. Combine the corn oil and water and mix well. Combine the dry ingredients with the wet ingredients and again mix well. Transfer the dough to a floured board and knead until it no longer sticks to your fingers. Using a rolling pin lightly dusted with flour, roll the dough out in a large square approximately 1/8 inch thick. Sprinkle the sesame seeds evenly over the dough and roll the seeds lightly into the surface of the dough with the rolling pin. Cut into 2-inch squares and place the squares, well spaced, on greased or Teflon cookie sheets. Bake for 8 to 10 minutes in the preheated 425° oven. Remove from the oven and cool to room temperature before removing from the cookie sheet. Store in an airtight container.

GRAHAM CRACKERS

3/4 cup graham flour
1/2 cup all-purpose flour
2 tablespoons honey
2-1/2 tablespoons corn oil
2 tablespoons water
1 teaspoon vanilla extract

Makes 26 crackers
2 crackers contain approximately:
1 starch portion
70 calories
Trace mg. sodium

Preheat the oven to 425°. Mix together the graham flour and all-purpose flour. Combine the honey, corn oil, water and vanilla extract and mix well. Combine the dry ingredients with the wet ingredients and again mix well. Transfer the dough to a floured board and knead until it no longer sticks to your fingers. Using a rolling pin lightly dusted with flour, roll the dough out in a large square approximately 1/8 inch thick. Cut into 2-inch squares and place the squares, well spaced, on greased or Teflon cookie sheets. Bake for 8 to 10 minutes in the preheated 425° oven. Remove from the oven and cool to room temperature before removing from the cookie sheet. Store in an airtight container.

TOASTED TORTILLA TRIANGLES

12 corn tortillas

Makes 72 tortilla triangles
6 triangles contain approximately:

1 starch portion
70 calories
Trace mg. sodium

Preheat the oven to 400°. Cut each tortilla into 6 pie-shaped wedges. Spread the tortilla pieces evenly on 2 cookie sheets and bake them in the preheated 400° oven for 10 minutes. Remove from the oven and turn each one over, placing them back in the oven for 3 to 5 more minutes, or until crisp and lightly browned. Remove from the oven and cool to room temperature.

I don't like to make any more tortilla triangles than I am planning to use immediately, because they are so much better freshly toasted. The advantage in making your own tortilla chips is that they are salt free and taste much fresher and better than those packaged salty chips you buy at the market. They are also fat free and lower in calories.

Variations Sprinkle the tortilla chips with ground cumin, chili powder, garlic powder or onion powder.

GIANT POPOVERS

4 egg whites, at room temperature
1 cup low-sodium low-fat milk, at
   room temperature
1 cup all-purpose flour
2 tablespoons unsalted butter or corn oil
   margarine, melted

Makes 6 popovers
1 popover contains approximately:
1 fat portion
1 starch portion
115 calories
35 mg. sodium

Preheat the oven to 450°. Put all ingredients in a blender container and blend at medium speed 15 seconds. *Do not overmix.* Pour the batter into 6 3-1/2-inch custard cups that have been well sprayed with a non-stick coating. (Only non-stick spray will prevent the popovers from sticking; butter or margarine won't do the job.) Bake in the 450° oven for 20 minutes. Reduce heat to 350° and bake for 20 more minutes.

    These enormous, delicious popovers will amaze and delight your friends, plus I have a sensational tip for you. Cool them to room temperature, wrap them carefully and tightly with foil or plastic wrap and freeze them. When you want to serve them, remove them from the freezer, unwrap, and place on a cookie sheet in a preheated 350° oven for about 12 to 15 minutes. You can then serve hot, gorgeous popovers to your guests without any of them ever realizing that you made them days ahead of time.

Giant Cinnamon Popovers Variation Add 1/4 teaspoon fructose and 1/2 teaspoon ground cinnamon to the blender container with the other ingredients. Proceed as directed.

WHOLE WHEAT WAFFLES

1 cup low-sodium low-fat milk, heated to
   lukewarm (110° to 115°)
2 teaspoons fresh lemon juice
1 envelope (1 tablespoon) active dry yeast
   (check date on package)
3 eggs, beaten
2 tablespoons corn oil

2 cups whole wheat flour, sifted

Makes 8 waffles
1 waffle contains approximately:
2-1/2 starch portions
175 calories
26 mg. sodium

Combine the milk with the lemon juice. Mix in the yeast and let stand in a warm place for a few minutes. Combine the eggs and the oil and add them to the yeast mixture. Stir in the flour, a little at a time, blending well. Cover the bowl with a tea towel and allow to rise in a warm place for approximately 1 hour. Bake in a preheated oiled or Teflon waffle iron.

This unsweetened waffle is good served with cheese sauce as well as the more classic sweet toppings.

PANCAKES

2 eggs
1/4 teaspoon potassium bicarbonate
4 teaspoons low-sodium baking powder
1/8 teaspoon dry mustard
1 cup low-sodium low-fat milk
1 teaspoon fresh lemon juice
1 cup all-purpose flour

1 teaspoon unsalted butter or corn oil
 margarine

Makes 16 4-inch pancakes
2 pancakes contain approximately:
1-1/4 starch portions
88 calories
17 mg. sodium

Beat the eggs, potassium bicarbonate, low-sodium baking powder and dry mustard until frothy. Combine the milk and lemon juice and mix well. Add the milk to the egg mixture and mix well. Stir in the flour, a little at a time.

Heat a cured iron skillet or Teflon pan until hot. Add the butter or margarine and when it melts, wipe it out, using a paper towel. Using a soup ladle, pour about 2 to 3 tablespoons batter in the pan for each pancake. Cook the pancakes over medium heat until the little bubbles that form on the surface of them burst. Then turn the pancakes over and brown the other side.

Remove to a warmed plate and repeat until all the batter is used. I like pancakes served with sour cream and fresh fruit better than with butter and maple syrup. Also, they are lower in calories when served this way.

CRÊPES

1 cup low-sodium low-fat milk
3/4 cup all-purpose flour
2 eggs, lightly beaten
1 teaspoon unsalted butter or corn oil
   margarine

Makes 12 crêpes
1 crêpe contains approximately:
3/4 starch portion
53 calories
11 mg. sodium

Put the milk and flour in a bowl and beat with an egg beater or a wire whisk until well mixed. Beat in the eggs and mix well.

   In a 6- or 7-inch cured iron omelet or crêpe pan, melt the butter or margarine over medium heat. When the butter is melted and the pan is hot, tilt the pan to coat the entire inner surface of the pan, then pour the remaining butter into the crêpe batter and mix well. Pour in just enough crêpe batter to barely cover the bottom of the pan (about 2 tablespoons) and tilt the pan from side to side to spread the batter evenly. When the edges of the crêpe start to curl, carefully turn it with a spatula and brown the other side. To keep the crêpes pliable, stack them in a covered casserole in a warm oven as they are cooked.

   I often make crêpes and freeze them. To do this, put a piece of foil or waxed paper between each crêpe and wrap well so that they are not exposed to the air. Before using, bring to room temperature and put in a preheated 300° oven for 20 minutes so they are soft and pliable.

GNOCCHI

2 medium potatoes (1 pound), boiled and
   mashed
1 egg, lightly beaten
1 cup all-purpose flour
2 tablespoons freshly grated Romano cheese
1/8 teaspoon garlic powder
1 teaspoon olive oil
1/4 teaspoon garlic powder
2 tablespoons unsalted butter or corn oil
   margarine, melted

Additional 1/4 cup freshly grated Romano
   cheese

Makes 12 servings (24 gnocchi)
Each serving contains approximately:
3/4 starch portion
1/2 fat portion
1/4 high-fat protein portion
100 calories
37 mg. sodium

Make certain the potatoes are mashed to a completely smooth consistency. I usually use a ricer or electric mixer to make them smooth. Place the mashed potatoes in a large bowl and make a well in the center. Pour the egg into the well and mix with the potatoes. Combine the flour, 2 tablespoons Romano cheese and 1/8 teaspoon of garlic powder and mix well. Gradually add the flour mixture, a little at a time. When the dough becomes stiff, turn it onto a lightly floured board and knead in the remaining flour mixture just as you would with bread, adding a little more flour, if necessary. The dough should be smooth but not sticky. Divide the dough into 2 sections. Roll each section into a long cylinder about 1 inch in diameter and cut the cylinders into 1-inch pieces. Press each piece of dough with your thumb to form a hollow spot in the top.

Preheat the oven to 350°. Fill a large pot with water, add the olive oil and 1/4 teaspoon garlic powder to the pot and bring to a rapid boil. Drop the gnocchi, a few at a time, into the water. Cook until they float to the top, then remove from the water with a slotted spoon, drain well and place in a flat baking dish in one layer. Put 1/4 teaspoon of the melted butter or margarine over the top of each one and sprinkle the additional grated Romano cheese evenly over the top of all of the gnocchi. Place in the preheated 350° oven for 15 minutes. If the cheese is not lightly browned, place under the broiler for 1 or 2 minutes to lightly brown the cheese before serving.

OVERNIGHT OATMEAL
(a new cold breakfast experience)

2 cups old-fashioned rolled oats
1/2 cup chopped almonds
1 cup chopped raisins
1 teaspoon ground cinnamon
3 cups water

Makes 5 cups
1/2 cup contains approximately:
1 starch portion
1 fruit portion
1/2 fat portion
133 calories
5 mg. sodium

Combine all the ingredients, except the water, in a mixing bowl and mix well. Add the water, mix well again, cover and refrigerate overnight before serving. It is even better if you wait 2 or 3 days before serving.

This is not only the easiest oatmeal recipe to prepare, but in my opinion, it is also the best tasting. It is delicious served with milk or yogurt, or even with cottage cheese and sliced fruit.

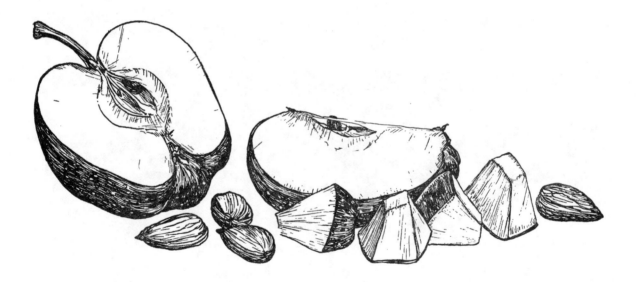

MATZO BALLS

2 eggs, lightly beaten
1 tablespoon corn oil
1/4 teaspoon onion powder
1/8 teaspoon white pepper
1/8 teaspoon ground nutmeg
1/2 cup matzo meal
2 to 3 quarts Unsalted Chicken Stock, page
   34, for cooking and/or serving

Makes 12 matzo balls
2 matzo balls contain approximately:
1 starch portion
70 calories
20 mg. sodium

Combine the eggs, corn oil, onion powder, white pepper and nutmeg and mix well. Slowly fold the matzo meal into the liquid mixture, being careful not to overmix. Cover and allow to stand for 2 hours—*but no longer than 2 hours.* Then moisten your fingers and form the dough into 12 walnut-sized balls.

Bring the chicken stock to a boil and place the matzo balls carefully into the stock. Lower the heat, cover and simmer for 30 minutes. If you are going to serve the matzo balls in the stock, divide the stock into soup bowls and place 1 or 2 matzo balls in each bowl. If you are using the matzo balls for some other dish, such as Matzo Balls Au Gratin, remove them from the stock with a slotted spoon.

CROÛTONS AND BREAD CRUMBS

4 slices dry low-sodium bread

Makes 2 cups croûtons
1/2 cup contains approximately:
1 starch portion
70 calories
7 mg. sodium

Makes about 1/2 cup bread crumbs
   (depending on how finely ground)
2 tablespoons contain approximately:
1 starch portion
70 calories
7 mg. sodium

To make croûtons: If you do not have any dry bread, separate slices of fresh bread and leave them on a counter top for several hours, turning occasionally, until they can be diced easily. Slice the bread in 1/4-inch cubes, place the cubes in a large shallow pan or on a cookie sheet and put them in a preheated 300° oven for about 20 minutes, or until a golden brown. Stir them occasionally so that they will brown evenly.

To make bread crumbs: Dry the bread for 2 or 3 days until it is very hard. Break it into pieces, put it in a blender container and grind to make bread crumbs. If you prefer toasted bread crumbs, toast the bread as directed for croûtons and then put the bread in the blender.

sweets and desserts

Amazingly enough, desserts, which create the greatest problem in most modified diet programs, actually present the least problem in a low-sodium diet. Fruits tend to have a lower sodium content than any other food, and fresh fruit is certainly the healthiest and one of the most delicious desserts available on any diet program. For this reason I have tried to keep this section limited to spectacular additions to your own dessert recipe repertoire, and have included some unusual low-sodium sauces for fresh fruits.

SPICED WALNUTS

1/2 cup fructose	Makes 2 cups
1/2 cup cornstarch	5 walnut halves contain approximately:
4 teaspoons ground cinnamon	1 fat portion
1 teaspoon ground allspice	1/4 fruit portion
1/2 teaspoon ground nutmeg	55 calories
1/4 teaspoon ground ginger	8 mg. sodium
2 egg whites	
2 cups walnut halves	

Preheat the oven to 250°. Sift together the fructose, cornstarch, cinnamon, allspice, nutmeg and ginger into a bowl. Mix well and set aside. Lightly beat the egg whites in a bowl. Add the walnuts and mix well. Coat each walnut with the fructose-spice mixture and shake off any excess dry mixture. Place, well spaced, on a well-oiled or Teflon cookie sheet. Bake in the preheated 250° oven for 1-1/2 hours. Remove the walnuts from the oven, let cool and store in a tightly covered container.

I have purposely made this recipe for a rather large quantity. This way you can wrap a cup of them in a decorative fashion and take them to a party as a host or hostess gift.

Variations This recipe can be made with other types of nuts. You can also mix these spiced nuts with raisins for a tasty snack. When adding raisins, remember that 2 tablespoons of raisins contain 40 calories, 1 fruit portion and 6 mg. of sodium.

FRUITY GRANOLA

1/4 cup corn oil
1/2 cup fructose
1 teaspoon vanilla extract
3-1/2 cups old-fashioned rolled oats
1/2 cup whole almonds
1/4 cup sunflower seeds
1/4 cup raisins
1/4 cup chopped pitted prunes
1/4 cup chopped dried apricots

Makes 6 cups
1/4 cup contains approximately:
1/2 fat portion
1/2 starch portion
3/4 fruit portion
88 calories
4 mg. sodium

Preheat the oven to 325°. Combine the corn oil, fructose and vanilla extract and mix well. Add all remaining ingredients, except the raisins, prunes and apricots, and mix well. Spread the mixture evenly on a cookie sheet with sides or in a baking dish and bake for 15 minutes in the preheated 325° oven. Remove from the oven and stir well. Continue baking for another 10 to 15 minutes or until lightly browned, stirring occasionally while cooking to brown evenly. Remove from the oven and mix with the raisins, prunes and apricots. Cool to room temperature and store in a tightly covered container.

BANANAS NORTH POLE

3 ripe bananas, sliced
1 teaspoon freshly grated orange peel for
   garnish
Fresh mint sprigs for garnish (optional)

Makes 4 servings
Each serving contains approximately:
1-1/2 fruit portions
60 calories
1 mg. sodium

Put the sliced bananas in a plastic bag in the freezer. When the bananas are completely frozen and hard, put them in a blender, a few at a time, and blend until smooth. Spoon the frozen puréed bananas into 4 sherbet glasses and garnish with freshly grated orange peel and fresh mint, if available.

This is an easy, delicious and dramatically beautiful dessert that is both low in sodium and high in potassium.

Variations Rather than grated orange peel you may wish to sprinkle each serving with a touch of ground cinnamon, nutmeg or anything else that contains few calories and milligrams of sodium and sounds good.

POACHED PEARS

6 firm ripe pears (Bartletts are best)
4 cups water
1 tablespoon vanilla extract
1/2 cup fructose
1 teaspoon ground cinnamon
Ground nutmeg for garnish (optional)

Makes 6 servings
Each serving contains approximately:
1-1/4 fruit portions
50 calories
3 mg. sodium

Peel pears carefully, leaving the stems on them. With an apple corer remove the core from the end opposite the stem. Put the water, vanilla extract, fructose and cinnamon in a saucepan and bring to a slow boil. Place the pears in the simmering water and cook, turning frequently, about 10 minutes, or until easily pierced with a fork but not soft. Remove from heat and let cool to room temperature in the sauce. Cover and refrigerate all day or overnight in the sauce.

Place each pear on a plate or in a shallow bowl and serve either plain with just a little nutmeg sprinkled over the top or with Low-Cholesterol Zabaglione, the Amaretto sauce used with Amaretto Peaches, or a little Vanilla Yogurt spooned over the top of them.

AMARETTO PEACHES

1 cup low-sodium low-fat milk
1 tablespoon cornstarch
1 tablespoon fructose
1-1/2 teaspoons vanilla extract
3 tablespoons Amaretto
2 egg whites, at room temperature
6 medium peaches, peeled and sliced (when
    fresh peaches are not available, canned
    peaches in water or natural juice may
    be used)

Makes 6 servings
Each serving contains approximately:
1-1/2 fruit portions
60 calories
20 mg. sodium

Put the milk in a saucepan. Add the cornstarch and fructose and stir until the cornstarch is thoroughly dissolved. Place the pan on low heat and slowly bring to a boil. Simmer, stirring constantly with a wire whisk, until slightly thickened. Remove the pan from the heat and allow to cool to room temperature. Add the vanilla extract and Amaretto liqueur and mix thoroughly. Beat the egg whites until stiff but not dry and fold them into the sauce. Divide the sliced peaches into 6 sherbet glasses or serving dishes and spoon 1/4 cup of the sauce over each serving.

BLUEBERRY MOUSSE

Mousse

2 envelopes (2 scant tablespoons) unflavored
   gelatin
1/4 cup cold water
1/4 cup boiling water
3 cups fresh or unsweetened frozen
   blueberries
1 8-ounce can crushed pineapple
   in natural juice, undrained
1 teaspoon vanilla extract
2 tablespoons fructose
1/2 cup sour cream

Sauce

1/2 cup sour cream
1-1/2 teaspoons fructose
1/2 teaspoon vanilla extract
Fresh mint sprigs for garnish (optional)

Makes 6 servings
Each serving contains approximately:
1-3/4 fruit portions
1-1/4 fat portions
126 calories
19 mg. sodium

Soften the gelatin in the cold water and allow to stand for 5 minutes. Add the boiling water and stir until the gelatin is completely dissolved. Put 2 cups of the blueberries in a blender container and set the remaining cup aside to add later. Add the gelatin mixture, crushed pineapple and its juice, vanilla extract, fructose and sour cream to the blueberries in the blender and blend until smooth. Pour the mixture into a bowl, add the remaining blueberries and mix well. Spoon into 6 small soufflé dishes or one large dessert dish. (This is also pretty done in a decorative mold.) Chill until firm.

Just before serving, make the sauce. Combine the sour cream, fructose and vanilla extract and mix with a wire whisk. Spoon some of the sauce over the top of each serving of mousse and garnish with a sprig of mint.

STRAWBERRIES HOFFMANN-LA ROCHE

1 cup low-sodium low-fat milk
1 tablespoon cornstarch
2 tablespoons fructose
1-1/2 teaspoons vanilla extract
2 tablespoons Grand Marnier
2 egg whites, at room temperature
1/8 teaspoon cream of tartar
4 cups sliced fresh strawberries

8 whole strawberries

Makes 8 servings
Each serving contains approximately:
1 starch portion
70 calories
15 mg. sodium

Put the milk in a saucepan. Add the cornstarch and fructose and stir until the cornstarch is thoroughly dissolved. Place the pan on low heat and bring to a boil. Simmer, stirring constantly with a wire whisk, until slightly thickened. Remove from the heat and cool to room temperature. Add the vanilla extract and Grand Marnier to the cooled sauce and mix well. Combine the egg whites and cream of tartar and beat until stiff but not dry. Fold the beaten egg whites into the sauce, then combine the sauce and the sliced strawberries and mix well. Divide evenly into 8 sherbet glasses. Place a whole strawberry on top of each serving for garnish.

I created this dessert for a dinner party given by Hoffmann-La Roche, Inc., at Joseph's Restaurant in Boston. It is not only beautiful and delicious but it is also very low in sodium.

LOW-CHOLESTEROL ZABAGLIONE

2 cups low-sodium low-fat milk
2 tablespoons cornstarch
3 tablespoons fructose
1 tablespoon vanilla extract
1/3 cup Marsala
5 egg whites, at room temperature

Makes 4 cups
1/2 cup contains approximately:
3/4 fruit portion
1/2 low-fat protein portion
1/4 low-fat milk portion
90 calories
33 mg. sodium

Put the milk in a saucepan. Add the cornstarch and fructose and stir until the cornstarch is thoroughly dissolved. Place the pan on low heat and slowly bring to a boil. Simmer, stirring constantly with a wire whisk, until slightly thickened. Remove from the heat, add the vanilla extract and Marsala wine and mix thoroughly. Beat the egg whites until stiff but not dry and fold into the sauce.

This can be served warm in sherbet glasses or used as a sauce over cakes, pies and fresh fruits. It is also good chilled and served either by itself or as a cold sauce.

OVERNIGHT NON-FAT YOGURT

1-1/2 cups low-sodium non-fat powdered milk
4 tablespoons low-fat plain yogurt
3-3/4 cups lukewarm water (110° to 115°)

1/2 cup contains approximately:
1 non-fat milk portion
80 calories
10 mg. sodium

Makes 4 cups

For your yogurt to incubate properly, it will need to be in an environment with a steady temperature of between 110° to 115°. If you have a gas oven, the heat of the pilot light will be sufficient. If you have an electric oven, you can preheat it to 120° and then turn it off when you put the yogurt in. A third possibility is to use a wide-mouth thermos, rinsed with warm water.

Combine all ingredients in a 1-quart glass baking dish. Place, uncovered, in an oven, as described above, or transfer to a thermos that has been rinsed with warm water and cover tightly.

Time will do the rest; it should take anywhere from 4 to 6 hours to overnight. Place the yogurt in a container with a tight-fitting lid and store in the refrigerator.

Repeat the process when your supply runs low, using 4 tablespoons of your own Overnight Non-fat Yogurt to make the new supply. (You have to start with low-fat yogurt from your grocery store, so the first batch will not be as absolutely non-fat as the following batches will be.) About every fourth time you make yogurt, use commercial low-fat plain yogurt for the starter or your yogurt will be too liquidy and too bland in taste.

Vanilla Yogurt Variation Add 1 teaspoon fructose and 1 teaspoon vanilla extract to the milk mixture.

FAST FROZEN YOGURT

1 envelope (1 scant tablespoon) unflavored gelatin	3 cups crushed ice
2 tablespoons cold water	Makes 4 cups
1/4 cup boiling water	1/2 cup contains approximately:
1-1/2 cups low-fat plain yogurt	1/4 low-fat milk portion
1/4 cup low-sodium non-fat powdered milk	1/2 fruit portion
1/4 cup fructose	52 calories
1-1/2 teaspoons vanilla extract	23 mg. sodium

Soften the gelatin in the cold water and allow to stand for 5 minutes. Add the boiling water and stir until the gelatin is completely dissolved. Cool to room temperature. Combine the gelatin-water mixture with the yogurt and mix well. Refrigerate until firmly jelled.

Combine the jelled yogurt, milk powder, fructose, vanilla extract and crushed ice in the blender and blend until smooth.

This is a sensational-tasting, soft frozen yogurt. Because the yogurt has never actually been frozen and processed, all of the valuable bacteria in it are still alive. You will find that this sensational-tasting dessert is also a great deal less expensive when you make it yourself. You must serve it immediately, however. The taste diminishes rapidly and the good bacteria are killed off when it is frozen, and it becomes watery when stored in the refrigerator.

COLD ORANGE SOUFFLÉ

2 envelopes (2 scant tablespoons) unflavored
   gelatin
1 cup cold water
2 egg yolks, at room temperature
2 6-ounce cans frozen unsweetened
   orange juice concentrate, thawed
1 teaspoon vanilla extract
8 egg whites, at room temperature
1/2 cup fructose
1 cup skimmed evaporated milk, chilled

Additional 1-1/2 tablespoons fructose
1 tablespoon freshly grated orange peel for
   garnish

Makes 16 servings
Each serving contains approximately:
1-1/4 fruit portions
1/2 low-fat protein portion
78 calories
46 mg. sodium

Soften the gelatin in the cold water and allow to stand for 5 minutes. Beat the egg yolks with a mixer or wire whisk until they are thick and foamy. Beat in the softened gelatin. Pour the mixture into a saucepan and place over moderate heat. Cook, stirring constantly, until thick enough to lightly coat a metal spoon. *Do not allow the mixture to come to a boil.* Remove the pan from the heat and stir in the thawed orange juice concentrate and vanilla extract. Pour the mixture into a large mixing bowl and refrigerate until thickened to a syrupy consistency, about 20 minutes.

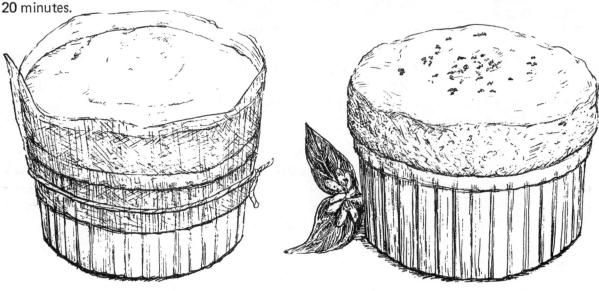

Beat the egg whites until they are frothy. Slowly add 1/2 cup fructose and continue beating until the egg whites are stiff but not dry; set aside. In another bowl, beat the chilled milk until it has doubled in volume. Slowly beat in 1-1/2 tablespoons fructose. Fold the whipped milk-fructose mixture gently but thoroughly into the orange juice mixture, using a rubber spatula. Fold in the egg whites, folding until no streaks of white show. Make a double-thickness waxed paper collar that will fit around the rim of a 7-1/2-inch (1-1/2-quart) soufflé dish. It should be wide enough to rise about 2 inches above the rim of the dish. Secure the collar to the dish with tape or string and then pour the soufflé mixture into the dish. Refrigerate for at least 4 hours before removing the collar and serving the soufflé. Lightly sprinkle the top with grated orange peel for garnish.

This is a dramatic dessert that can be made ahead of time. I created the recipe for "Menu Magic," a product book for SweetLite fructose, and asked their permission to reprint it here not only because it's beautiful and delicious, but also because it's appropriate for low-sodium diets.

NOODLE PUDDING

1/2 cup chopped walnuts
4 cups cooked noodles (7 ounces dry)
1/3 cup fructose
3/4 teaspoon ground cinnamon
1 tablespoon vanilla extract
1/2 cup raisins
3 medium green apples, cored and thinly
   sliced
2 eggs, lightly beaten

1/4 cup unsalted butter or corn oil margarine,
   melted

Makes 12 servings
Each serving contains approximately:
3/4 starch portion
1-1/4 fat portions
1 fruit portion
149 calories
13 mg. sodium

Preheat the oven to 375°. Place the walnuts on a cookie sheet in the preheated 375° oven for approximately 8 minutes or until golden brown. Watch them carefully as they burn easily. (Leave the oven on.) Combine the walnuts, cooked noodles and all remaining ingredients, except the butter or margarine, and mix thoroughly. Transfer the mixture to a 2-quart casserole or baking dish and pour the melted butter or margarine evenly over the top. Bake in the preheated 375° oven for 45 minutes.

JAMAICAN RICE PUDDING WITH RUM SAUCE

4 small bananas, mashed
2 cups low-sodium low-fat milk
4 eggs, lightly beaten
1/4 cup fructose
1/8 teaspoon ground ginger
1 tablespoon ground cinnamon
2 teaspoons vanilla extract
1 teaspoon rum extract
2 cups cooked long-grain white rice
1 cup Jamaican Rum Sauce, following

Makes 8 servings
Each serving with sauce contains
   approximately:
1/4 fat portion
1/2 starch portion
1/4 low-fat milk portion
1/2 medium-fat protein portion
1-1/2 fruit portions
175 calories
35 mg. sodium

Preheat the oven to 350°. Combine all ingredients, except the rice and sauce, and mix well. Add the rice and again mix well. Pour into a 2-quart casserole and set the casserole in a larger deep pan with boiling water to a depth of 1 inch. Bake in the preheated 350° oven for 1 hour and 20 minutes. Serve warm with 2 tablespoons of Jamaican Rum Sauce on each serving.

JAMAICAN RUM SAUCE

1 tablespoon unsalted butter or corn oil
   margarine
1 tablespoon all-purpose flour
1 cup boiling water
2 tablespoons fructose
1/2 teaspoon ground cinnamon
1-1/2 teaspoons vanilla extract
3/4 teaspoon rum extract

Makes 1 cup sauce
2 tablespoons contain approximately:
1/2 fruit portion
1/4 fat portion
31 calories
Trace mg. sodium

Melt the butter or margarine in a saucepan. Add the flour all at once and cook, stirring constantly, for at least 3 minutes. Remove the pan from the heat and add the boiling water all at once, stirring with a wire whisk. Add the fructose and cinnamon to the pan and return the pan to the heat. Simmer, stirring constantly with a wire whisk, until the sauce is slightly thickened. Remove the pan from the heat and mix in the vanilla and rum extracts. Serve warm or cold.

CRÊPES SUZETTE

1 cup fresh orange juice
2 teaspoons cornstarch
3 tablespoons fructose
1 tablespoon freshly grated orange peel
1/4 cup orange liqueur
1 tablespoon unsalted butter or corn oil
   margarine
12 Crêpes, page 148, warmed
2 tablespoons brandy (optional)

Makes 6 servings
Each serving contains approximately:
1 starch portion
1-1/4 fruit portions
1/2 fat portion
143 calories
23 mg. sodium

Pour the orange juice into a saucepan. Add the cornstarch and 2 tablespoons of the fructose and stir until the cornstarch is dissolved. Slowly bring the mixture to a boil and simmer, stirring constantly with a wire whisk, until slightly thickened. Remove the pan from the heat and add the grated orange peel, orange liqueur and butter or margarine. Stir until the butter or margarine has completely melted and then pour into a heated chafing dish. Dip both sides of each crêpe in the sauce and fold it in half and then in half again, forming a triangle. Push the folded crêpe to the side of the chafing dish and continue until all the crêpes have been dipped and folded, gradually arranging them on a warmed serving plate as they become crowded in the dish. Sprinkle the remaining tablespoon of fructose evenly over the crêpes.

   If you wish, at this point you can add brandy to the sauce remaining in the chafing dish and ignite it with a match. Shake the chafing dish gently back and forth while you spoon the flaming liquid over the folded crêpes until the flame goes out.

CREAM PUFFS

1/2 cup water
4 tablespoons unsalted butter or corn oil
   margarine
1/2 cup all-purpose flour
2 teaspoons fructose
2 eggs

Makes 8 unfilled cream puffs
Each puff contains approximately:
1/4 medium-fat protein portion
1/2 starch portion
1-1/2 fat portions
122 calories
16 mg. sodium

Preheat the oven to 375°. Combine the water and butter or margarine in a saucepan and bring to a boil. Combine the flour and fructose and add all at once to the boiling liquid. Mix well and beat over low heat until the mixture leaves the sides of the pan and forms a compact ball. Remove from the heat and cool slightly, about 5 minutes. Add the eggs, one at a time, beating well after each addition. Continue beating until the mixture has a satinlike sheen.

Grease a large baking sheet and arrange the batter in 8 equal mounds about 2 inches apart, making a pattern on the top of each mound. Bake in the preheated 375° oven for 40 to 45 minutes, or until nicely browned and puffy. Remove from the oven and immediately cut a slit in the side of each puff. Return to the oven for 8 to 10 more minutes. Remove from the oven and cool on a cake rack. To serve, split the cream puffs almost all of the way around or slice the top off of each puff and fill as desired.

GOLDEN CREAM PUFFS

1 6-ounce can frozen unsweetened orange
   juice concentrate, thawed
2 cups (1 pound) partially skimmed ricotta
   cheese, rinsed, page 178
1/4 cup fructose
1-1/2 teaspoons vanilla extract
8 Cream Puffs, preceding, cut in half
8 thin slices of orange (with peel) for garnish
   (optional)

Makes 8 servings
Each serving contains approximately:
1 low-fat protein portion
1/4 medium-fat protein portion
1-1/2 fat portions
1-1/4 fruit portions
1/2 starch portion
227 calories
63 mg. sodium

Combine all ingredients, except the cream puffs and garnish, in a large bowl. Using a wire whisk, beat until smooth and light in texture. Spoon the mixture evenly into the bottom halves of the 8 Cream Puffs. Place the top on each puff and garnish with an orange slice, if desired.

KUCHEN

Kuchen
1-1/2 cups all-purpose flour
4 teaspoons low-sodium baking powder
4 tablespoons unsalted butter or corn oil margarine
1/3 cup fructose
1 egg, lightly beaten
2/3 cup low-sodium low-fat milk
1/2 teaspoon almond extract
1-1/2 teaspoons vanilla extract

Streusel Topping
3 tablespoons fructose
1 tablespoon unsalted butter or corn oil margarine
2 tablespoons all-purpose flour
1/2 teaspoon ground cinnamon
1/4 cup finely ground or crushed almonds

Makes 12 servings
Each serving contains approximately:
1 starch portion
1-1/2 fat portions
3/4 fruit portion
168 calories
7 mg. sodium

Preheat the oven to 350°. To make the kuchen, sift together the flour and baking powder and set aside. In a large bowl, combine the butter or margarine and fructose and cream together until light. Add the egg, milk and almond and vanilla extracts and mix thoroughly. Add the flour mixture, a little at a time, mixing well. Stir the batter until smooth, then spread in a greased 9-inch cake pan.

To make the topping, mix the fructose, butter or margarine, cinnamon and flour together until a crumbly mixture is formed. Add the almonds and mix thoroughly. Sprinkle the streusel over the top of the kuchen and bake in the preheated 350° oven for about 30 minutes or until nicely browned.

DIETER'S DREAM FRUITCAKE

1 envelope (1 scant tablespoon) unflavored
  gelatin
2 tablespoons cold water
1/4 cup boiling water
1/2 cup low-sodium low-fat milk
1/2 cup unsweetened applesauce
1/2 cup raisins
1/2 teaspoon ground cinnamon
1/4 teaspoon ground allspice
1/8 teaspoon ground nutmeg
1/2 teaspoon carob powder or unsweetened
  cocoa powder

1 teaspoon vanilla extract
1 8-ounce can crushed pineapple
  in natural juice, drained
1/2 cup chopped walnuts

Makes 8 servings
Each serving contains approximately:
1 fruit portion
1/2 fat portion
63 calories
5 mg. sodium

Soften the gelatin in the cold water and allow to stand for 5 minutes. Add the boiling water and stir until the gelatin is completely dissolved. Pour the gelatin mixture and all remaining ingredients, except the crushed pineapple and walnuts, in a blender container. Blend until the ingredients are thoroughly mixed and the raisins are coarsely chopped. Pour the blended mixture into a bowl and add the drained crushed pineapple. Mix thoroughly. Pour the mixture into an oiled 9-inch cake pan and refrigerate until firm—several hours or overnight.

Just before serving, put the walnuts on a cookie sheet in a preheated 350° oven for 8 minutes or until golden brown. Watch them carefully as they burn easily. Remove the fruitcake from the refrigerator. Place a cake plate over the top of the cake pan and quickly invert the fruitcake onto the plate. Sprinkle the toasted walnuts evenly over the top.

CINNAMON-LEMON CHEESECAKE

1/2 cup graham cracker crumbs (8 graham crackers)

2 tablespoons unsalted butter or corn oil margarine, at room temperature

2 cups (1 pound) partially skimmed ricotta cheese, rinsed, page 178

1/3 cup fructose

2 tablespoons all-purpose flour

2 teaspoons ground cinnamon

2 egg yolks, at room temperature

1/2 cup skimmed evaporated milk

2 teaspoons vanilla extract

2 teaspoons freshly grated lemon peel

3 egg whites, at room temperature

1/8 teaspoon cream of tartar

Makes 12 servings
Each serving contains approximately:
3/4 low-fat protein portion
1/4 starch portion
1/2 fat portion
1/2 fruit portion
103 calories
88 mg. sodium

Preheat the oven to 325°. Combine the graham cracker crumbs and butter or margarine and mix well. Press the mixture evenly into the bottom of a well-greased (or Teflon) 9-inch cake pan and set aside. Combine the ricotta cheese, fructose, flour, cinnamon, egg yolks, milk, vanilla extract and lemon peel in a blender container and blend to a smooth, creamy consistency. Pour the mixture into a large mixing bowl and set aside.

In another bowl, combine the egg whites and cream of tartar and beat until stiff but not dry. Fold the beaten egg whites into the cheese mixture and pour the batter over the graham cracker crust in the cake pan. Bake in the center of the preheated 325° oven for 45 to 50 minutes. Remove from the oven and cool on a cake rack. Loosen the sides of the cheesecake from the pan with the tip of a sharp knife. Then place a plate over the top of the cake pan and quickly invert the cake onto the plate. Cover and chill before serving.

The graham cracker crust makes a beautiful topping for this cheesecake. In fact, it is so pretty I often decorate it with fresh fruit and candles for a birthday cake.

PERFECT SALT-FREE PIE CRUST

1 cup whole-wheat pastry flour
1/4 cup corn oil
3 tablespoons ice water
1/4 teaspoon cider vinegar

Makes 1 9-inch pie crust

1 pie crust contains approximately:
5-1/4 starch portions
12 fat portions
908 calories
5 mg. sodium

Put the flour into a 9-inch pie pan. Measure the oil in a large measuring cup, add the ice water and vinegar and mix well, using a fork. Slowly add the liquid to the flour in the pie pan, mixing it with the fork. Continue mixing until all ingredients are well blended. Press into shape with your fingers, making sure the crust covers the entire inner surface of the pan evenly. If the recipe calls for a prebaked crust, prick the bottom of the crust with a fork in several places and place in a preheated 375° oven for 20 to 25 minutes, or until a golden brown.

I discovered this method for making pie crust while working on the *Fabulous Fiber Cookbook.* The recipe will continue to appear in my future books because it is the easiest, least messy method for making a good pie crust I have ever found. This is also the reason I titled it "perfect."

PEANUT BUTTER-HONEY PIE

1 envelope (1 scant tablespoon) unflavored
   gelatin
2 tablespoons cold water
1/4 cup boiling water
1-1/2 cups low-sodium low-fat milk
1/2 cup unsalted peanut butter
3 tablespoons honey
1-1/2 teaspoons vanilla extract
1 Perfect Salt-Free Pie Crust, preceding,
   prebaked

Ground cinnamon for garnish

Makes 8 servings
Each serving contains approximately:
1/2 fruit portion
1-1/4 starch portions
1/2 high-fat protein portion
1-1/2 fat portions
224 calories
6 mg. sodium

Soften the gelatin in the cold water and allow to stand for 5 minutes. Add the boiling water and stir until the gelatin is completely dissolved. Put the gelatin mixture into a blender container and add the milk, peanut butter, honey and vanilla extract. Blend until smooth and frothy. Pour the mixture into the prebaked pie shell and sprinkle the top lightly with cinnamon. Refrigerate until firm before serving.

This pie is my favorite dessert. Anyone familiar with my other cookbooks knows, however, how much I love peanut butter—just plain, in punch, cookies and salad dressing, as well as in pie.

PERFECT PUMPKIN PIE

1/4 cup chopped walnuts
1 envelope (1 scant tablespoon) unflavored
   gelatin
2 tablespoons cold water
1/4 cup boiling water
2 cups mashed cooked pumpkin (1 16-ounce
   can)
1-1/2 teaspoons ground cinnamon
1/2 teaspoon ground ginger
1/4 teaspoon ground cloves
1/4 cup fructose
2 teaspoons vanilla extract

1 cup low-sodium low-fat milk
1 Perfect Salt-Free Pie Crust, preceding,
   prebaked

Makes 8 servings
Each serving contains approximately:
1-1/4 starch portions
1/2 fruit portion
1-1/2 fat portions
176 calories
4 mg. sodium

Preheat the oven to 350°. Put the walnuts on a cookie sheet in the preheated 350° oven for about 8 minutes or until golden brown. Watch them carefully as they burn easily. Set aside.

Soften the gelatin in the cold water and allow to stand for 5 minutes. Add the boiling water and stir until the gelatin is completely dissolved. Put the gelatin mixture into a blender container and add all remaining ingredients, except the walnuts and crust. Blend until frothy. Let stand until slightly thickened before pouring into the baked pie shell. Refrigerate until firm. Sprinkle the toasted walnuts evenly over the top before serving.

I stole the title of my own pie crust for this pumpkin pie recipe because it is the fastest, easiest pumpkin pie to make I know of. It is also one of the most delicious, and is certainly lower in calories than any pumpkin pie I have ever eaten.

beverages

Every type of calorie counter will be happy with this beverage section. It has calorie-free Desert Tea for the "teatotaler" and a Counterfeit Cocktail for the cocktail party lover who can't afford the calories before dinner. For the wine connoisseur who enjoys a glass of wine or two with his dinner, but doesn't want the added calories or occasional aftereffect of the alcohol, there is a recipe for removing the alcohol so that you can enjoy wine with your dinner without worrying about a headache in the morning.

For those who want something a little more substantial to drink, there are many unusual, refreshing fruit drinks, plus there is a Vitality Cocktail for people who prefer to drink breakfast. Because my favorite beverage is Peanut Butter Punch in my *Fabulous Fiber Cookbook,* I have included a low-sodium variation of this all-American classic here.

VITALITY COCKTAIL
(a dynamic way to start the day)

1/2 cup fresh orange juice
1/2 cup low-sodium low-fat milk
1 egg (in the shell), dipped in boiling water
   for 30 seconds
1 tablespoon wheat germ
1 tablespoon unprocessed wheat bran
1 tablespoon brewer's yeast
1 teaspoon fructose
1/4 teaspoon vanilla extract
3 ice cubes, crushed

Makes 1 serving
Contains approximately:
1/2 low-fat milk portion
1-1/2 fruit portions
1 medium-fat protein portion
3/4 starch portion
252 calories
75 mg. sodium

Put all ingredients into a blender container and blend until smooth. This is a delicious high-protein, high-fiber, low-calorie, low-sodium beverage.

Variation Add fruits, such as peaches, bananas and apples, when available.

COUNTERFEIT COCKTAIL

Ice cubes
Perrier water or soda water
Fresh lime juice to taste
Angostura bitters

1 8-ounce serving contains approximately:
Calories and sodium negligible

This drink may be prepared in many different ways. I use a large wineglass, fill it with ice cubes and Perrier water and then add the juice of a quarter lime and about 2 dashes of Angostura bitters, or enough to make the drink a beautiful pale pink color. A Counterfeit Cocktail may, however, be served in a highball glass, a beer mug—use your imagination. It is a delightfully refreshing drink and most bars and cocktail lounges have all of the ingredients, so you can order it when you are dining out as well as prepare it in your own home. It has a decided advantage over most other non-alcoholic drinks in that it is not sweet, the calories are negligible and it is low in sodium.

CALORIE-COUNTER'S WINE
(drink without drinking)

Dry red, white or rosé wine (amount desired)

60 calories
4 mg. sodium

1 3-ounce serving contains approximately:

Pour the wine into a non-aluminum saucepan and bring to a slow boil. When the wine starts to boil, ignite it with a match and allow it to burn until the flame goes out, thus burning off all of the alcohol. I suggest holding the lighted match with kitchen tongs that are at least 8 inches long, so you are not putting your hand close to the boiling wine when igniting it. The volume of the wine will be reduced by the volume of the alcohol content of the wine. Allow the wine to cool to room temperature, then store tightly covered in the refrigerator.

Wine with the alcohol removed is certainly not an epicurean delight, and therefore I suggest using less expensive rather than valuable vintage wine for this purpose. Removing the alcohol does, however, allow you to enjoy wine with your meals with reduced calories and no chance of a headache in the morning. Red wine is best served at room temperature and both white and rosé wines should be served chilled.

BLOODY MARY (WITH VODKA)
BLOODY SHAME (WITHOUT VODKA)

2 tablespoons fresh lime juice
4 teaspoons fructose
1/2 teaspoon freshly ground black pepper
1-1/2 cups unsalted V-8 Juice or tomato
   juice (1 12-ounce can)
4 to 6 drops Tabasco sauce, depending
   on hotness desired
6 tablespoons vodka (optional)
Ice cubes
Raw zucchini or cucumber sticks for
   garnish (optional)

Makes 2 servings
Each serving without vodka contains
   approximately:
3/4 fruit portion
1 vegetable portion
55 calories
55 mg. sodium

Each serving with vodka (90 proof)
   contains approximately:
3/4 fruit portion
1 vegetable portion
167 calories
55 mg. sodium

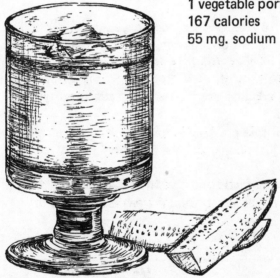

Mix together the lime juice, fructose and black pepper until the fructose is dissolved. Add the V-8 or tomato juice, Tabasco sauce and vodka, if using, and mix well. Pour over ice cubes in glasses and garnish with zucchini or cucumber sticks, if desired.

HOT DIGGITY DOG
(better than a salty dog)

2 cups fresh grapefruit juice
1/4 teaspoon fructose
Dash cayenne pepper
6 tablespoons vodka (optional)
1 lemon or lime
Fructose for garnishing glasses
Ice cubes

Makes 4 servings
Each serving without vodka contains
   approximately:

1 fruit portion
40 calories
1 mg. sodium

Each serving with vodka (90 proof) contains
   approximately:
1 fruit portion
96 calories
1 mg. sodium

Combine the grapefruit juice, 1/4 teaspoon fructose, cayenne pepper and vodka, if using, and mix thoroughly. Set aside. Cut the lemon or lime into 5 thin slices and rub the rims of 4 glasses with one of the slices. Make a thin layer of fructose on a plate and dip the rim of each glass into it, shaking off the excess. Slice halfway through the diameter of each remaining slice of lemon or lime and balance one on the edge of each glass. Fill each glass with ice cubes, then with the grapefruit juice, mix and serve.

This is a perfect drink for brunch. It is so tasty that many a salty dog lover has become a Hot Diggity Dog devotee after just one glass.

Note This drink tastes best when made with freshly squeezed grapefruit juice. Canned or frozen unsweetened grapefruit juice may be substituted if fresh is unavailable.

DESERT TEA

2 tea bags
2 quarts cold water

Makes 8 servings
Calories and sodium negligible

Put the tea bags in a 2-quart glass jar or bottle with a lid, fill with water and cover. Put the jar in the sun until the tea is the desired strength. This usually takes 2 hours, sometimes more, depending on the intensity of the sun. Remove the tea bags and store the tea in the refrigerator. This is the best iced tea imaginable.

Variation Add freshly grated orange peel or crushed mint leaves to the bottle with the tea bags.

FRESH FRUIT FRAPPE

1 banana, sliced
1 teaspoon fresh lemon juice
1 8-ounce can crushed pineapple
  in natural juice, undrained
1 cup fresh orange juice
1 cup low-sodium low-fat milk
1 teaspoon vanilla extract
4 ice cubes, crushed

Mint sprigs for garnish (optional)

Makes 4 servings
Each serving contains approximately:
1/4 low-fat milk portion
1-1/2 fruit portions
91 calories
4 mg. sodium

Put the banana and lemon juice in a blender container and blend until smooth. Add all remaining ingredients and blend until smooth and frothy. Pour into 4 chilled glasses and garnish with fresh mint, if available.

PEANUT BUTTER PUNCH

1 cup low-sodium low-fat milk
2 tablespoons unsalted peanut butter
1 tablespoon date "sugar," or
  2 dates, pitted and chopped
1 teaspoon vanilla extract
4 ice cubes, crushed
Ground cinnamon or nutmeg for garnish
  (optional)

Makes 2 servings
Each serving contains approximately:
1/2 low-fat milk portion
1/2 fruit portion
1/2 high-fat protein portion
131 calories
10 mg. sodium

Put all ingredients into a blender container and blend until smooth and creamy. Pour into 2 chilled glasses and sprinkle a little cinnamon or nutmeg on the top of each serving, if desired.

As I mentioned in the introduction to this chapter, this is a variation of a recipe that appeared in the *Fabulous Fiber Cookbook,* where I explained that I have long been a real "peanut butter addict." Now for all of you who share this feeling, I have come up with a way you can drink it—a delicious and unusual beverage not only high in protein, but also low in sodium.

Variation Omit the ice cubes and serve this hot for breakfast instead of cocoa.

PIÑA COLADA

1 cup low-sodium low-fat milk
2 cups unsweetened pineapple juice
1 teaspoon fructose
1 teaspoon vanilla extract
1/2 teaspoon coconut extract
2 ice cubes, crushed
Ice cubes for glasses

Makes 4 servings
Each serving contains approximately:
1-1/4 fruit portions
1/4 low-fat milk portion
81 calories
5 mg. sodium

Put all ingredients, except the ice cubes for the glasses, into a blender container and blend until smooth and frothy. Pour over ice cubes in 4 glasses.

HIGH-POTASSIUM PUNCH

1/2 cup chopped pitted dates
1 banana, sliced
2 cups low-sodium low-fat milk
1 teaspoon vanilla extract
4 ice cubes, crushed
Ground cinnamon or nutmeg for garnish
   (optional)

Makes 4 servings
Each serving contains approximately:
1-1/2 fruit portions
1/2 low-fat milk portion
123 calories
9 mg. sodium

Put all ingredients into a blender container and blend until smooth and creamy. Pour into 4 chilled glasses and sprinkle a little cinnamon or nutmeg on the top of each serving, if desired.

secret suggestions and important facts

LOW-SODIUM BAKING POWDER

Regular baking powder contains 40 milligrams of sodium per teaspoon, while low-sodium baking powder contains only one milligram per teaspoon. When using the latter, however, you will need to add half again as much (50 percent more) as you would if using regular baking powder. If you are unable to buy low-sodium baking powder, ask your druggist to make it for you, using the following formula:

Cornstarch	56.0 grams
Potassium bitartrate	112.25 grams
Potassium bicarbonate	79.5 grams
Tartaric acid	15.0 grams

POTASSIUM BICARBONATE

Potassium bicarbonate is substituted for baking soda in the low-sodium diet. The latter is sodium bicarbonate and contains 1,232 milligrams of sodium per teaspoon, while potassium bicarbonate contains no sodium. Most low-sodium cookbooks tell you to use potassium bicarbonate in the same amount as you would baking soda. I have found that it has a definite aftertaste when used in that quantity, and that half as much will give you the desired results in texture without the unpleasant flavor.

RINSING COTTAGE CHEESE

Commercial cottage cheese, while low in calories and high in protein, is also high in sodium. Rinsing the cottage cheese thoroughly in a strainer, sieve or cheesecloth reduces the sodium content greatly. There are two recipes for making your own low-sodium cottage cheese in this book and it is also possible to buy dry curd unsalted cottage cheese in many markets. Ricotta cheese is also high in sodium and may be rinsed by this same method.

EGGS

When using raw eggs or raw egg whites, it is important to coddle or dip the whole egg (in the shell) in boiling water for 30 seconds before using it. The reason for this is that the avedin, a component of raw egg whites, is believed to block the absorption of biotin, one of the water-soluble vitamins. Avedin is extremely sensitive to heat and coddling the egg inactivates it.

LOW-SODIUM MILK

The most generally available low-sodium milk nationally is Carnation Lo-Sodium Modified Milk. One cup contains 12.5 milligrams of sodium and 117 calories. Regular low-fat (two percent) milk contains approximately 150 milligrams of sodium and 125 calories per cup. Regular non-fat milk contains approximately 127 milligrams of sodium and 80 calories per cup.

When you consider that the number of calories saved by using non-fat milk instead of Carnation Lo-Sodium Modified Milk is only 37 per cup, but the savings on milligrams of sodium is 114.5 per cup, you can immediately see the importance of using low-sodium milk for both drinking and cooking. Even on very low-calorie and low-saturated-fat diets, the calories can be saved in other places where the sodium difference is not so great.

WINES

When using wine for cooking, never use wines labeled "cooking wine " because they contain salt. In fact, the reason for the term "cooking wine" goes back in history to a time when the wine for kitchen use was salted to prevent the cook from drinking it.

COMMERCIAL CONDIMENTS

I have recipes in this book for practically all of the low-sodium condiments and sauces available commercially, such as mustard, mayonnaise, catsup, salad dressings, etc. I have done this for three reasons: First, commercial low-sodium products are very expensive. Second, they are not always available in the markets. Third, even when they are available and you are willing to pay the prices asked, very few of them taste good. For this reason I want to help anyone on a sodium-restricted diet to become independent enough within the diet program prescribed to be able to create the necessary condiments in the kitchen.

BAKON YEAST

Bakon Yeast is dried torula yeast, and adds a marvelous smoked-baconlike flavor to breads, salad dressings, sauces and omelets. I often add it to unsalted butter or margarine for browning meats or for cooking vegetables. It is of vegetable origin, contains no sugar or salt and it is acceptable on the most severely restricted diets. The sodium content of Bakon Yeast is less than 10 milligrams of sodium per 100 grams, and one rounded teaspoonful, or 100 grams, contains only 12 calories.

FRUCTOSE

Fructose is a natural fruit sugar that is approximately one and one-half times sweeter than sucrose (ordinary table sugar). Because of this you use less of it, therefore automatically reducing the calories. I have found fructose to be the best flavor heightener in vegetable preparations when not using salt. I also routinely use it in small amounts in marinades even when the overall effect desired is not sweetness. This is because, in the absence of salt, fructose serves as a flavor heightener and sharpens the taste of the other ingredients.

SATURATED FAT CONTROL

To lower the amount of saturated fat in your diet, apply the following rules to your diet program:
1. Use liquid vegetable oils and margarines that are high in polyunsaturated fats instead of butter. Two of the best oils for this purpose are safflower oil and corn oil.
2. Do not use coconut oil or chocolate. Many non-dairy creamers and sour cream substitutes contain coconut oil. Use coconut extract and dry powdered cocoa.
3. Use non-fat milk, or low-sodium low-fat milk if on a low-sodium diet.
4. Avoid commercial ice cream.
5. Limit the amount of beef, lamb and pork in your diet to four or five times a week and eat fish, chicken, veal and white meat of turkey in their place.
6. Buy lean cuts of meat and trim all visible fat from them before cooking.

CHOLESTEROL CONTROL

To lower the amount of cholesterol in your diet, apply the following restrictions to your diet program:
1. Limit or avoid egg yolks.
2. Limit shellfish, such as oysters, clams, scallops, lobster, shrimp and crab.
3. Limit or avoid organ meats of all animals, such as liver, heart, kidney, sweetbreads and brains.

epilogue

In our culture, salt (sodium chloride) must be considered to be a condiment rather than a nutrient because we habitually ingest from five to fifty times our nutritional requirement. Salt even can be called a subtle form of poison, since there is accumulating evidence that in the amounts habitually ingested in America it probably is a major factor causing high blood pressure. Consider the following points:

1. When one relatively pure culture is compared with another with respect to the number of cases of high blood pressure, the higher the habitual salt intake of that culture the higher the incidence of high blood pressure.

2. In any culture where the habitual salt intake is less than 500 milligrams of sodium per day, the incidence of high blood pressure approaches zero.

3. Experiments in animals suggest that the ability to tolerate high salt diets without developing high blood pressure may be determined genetically. For some populations, salt remains a condiment and does not become a poison even in very large amounts. For others, chronic ingestion of even moderate amounts of salt eventually may cause high blood pressure.

4. A case in point may be the American Negro whose African ancestors as a cultural group through evolution may have become genetically intolerant to salt because of its scarcity in their environment. When in the 19th century these people were transported into the high-salt culture of North America, high blood pressure began to take its toll. Today high blood pressure is much more severe and much more common among American blacks than any other cultural sub-group in America.

Whether or not all of the above points are indeed valid, the fact remains that our culturally determined high salt intake is not in any way beneficial. Therefore, it seems reasonable to propose that if we as a people could learn to prefer less salt in our food, the number of cases of high blood pressure in future generations might decrease dramatically. To accomplish this goal, we should condition our infants to retain their instinctive dislike for salt. Salt should never be added in the preparation of commercial baby foods or to home-prepared foods. And foods such as ham and bacon, which are naturally high in salt, should be avoided altogether. If these three relatively simple steps were followed by America's parents, the chances would be excellent that habitual salt intake in our culture would be cut in half in one generation. That in turn might reduce the number of new cases of high blood pressure by tens of millions. As a result, there would be a dramatic reduction in the number of cases of stroke, heart attack and kidney failure.

Beginning now, an effort should be made through modification of the diet of our infant population to reduce the habitual salt intake of the American people. We have nothing to lose by such an undertaking, and the gains in terms of prevention of human suffering could be enormous.

BELDING H. SCRIBNER, M.D.
Professor and Head
Kidney Disease
Department of Medicine
University of Washington Hospital

equivalents

BEVERAGES

Ice cubes
2 ice cubes = 1/4 cup
8 ice cubes = 1 cup
Instant coffee
4-ounce jar = 60 cups coffee
Coffee
1 pound (80 tablespoons) = 40 to
    50 cups
Tea leaves
1 pound = 300 cups tea

FATS

Miscellaneous
Bacon, 1 pound, rendered = 1-1/2 cups
Bacon, 1 slice, cooked crisp =
    1 tablespoon, crumbled
Butter, 1 cube (1/4 pound) = 1/2 cup
    or 8 tablespoons
Cheese, cream, 3-ounce package =
    6 tablespoons
Cream, heavy whipping, 1 cup =
    2 cups, whipped
Margarine, 1 cube (1/4 pound) =
    1/2 cup or 8 tablespoons
Nuts in the shell
Almonds, 1 pound = 1 cup nutmeats
Brazil nuts, 1 pound = 1-1/2 cups
    nutmeats
Peanuts, 1 pound = 2 cups nutmeats
Pecans, 1 pound = 2-1/2 cups nutmeats
Walnuts, 1 pound = 2-1/2 cups
    nutmeats
Nuts, shelled
Almonds, 1/2 pound = 2 cups
Almonds, 42, chopped = 1/2 cup

Brazil nuts, 1/2 pound = 1-1/2 cups
Coconut, 1/2 pound, shredded =
    2-1/2 cups
Macadamia nuts, 3, finely
    chopped = 1 tablespoon
Peanuts, 1/2 pound = 1 cup
Peanuts, 50 chopped = 1/2 cup
Pecans, 1/2 pound = 2 cups
Pecans, 42 halves, chopped = 1/2 cup
Walnuts, 1/2 pound = 2 cups
Walnuts, 15 halves, chopped = 1/2 cup

FRUITS (DRIED)

Apricots, 24 halves, 1 cup = 1-1/2
    cups, cooked
Dates, 1 pound, 2-1/2 cups = 1-3/4
    cups, pitted and chopped
Figs, 1 pound, 2-1/2 cups = 4-1/4
    cups, cooked
Pears, 1 pound, 3 cups = 5-1/2 cups,
    cooked
Prunes, pitted, 1 pound, 2-1/2 cups =
    3-3/4 cups, cooked
Raisins, seedless, 1 pound, 2-3/4
    cups = 3-3/4 cups, cooked

FRUITS (FRESH)

Apples, 1 pound, 4 small = 3 cups,
    chopped
Apricots, 1 pound, 6 to 8 average =
    2 cups, chopped
Bananas, 1 pound, 4 small = 2 cups,
    mashed
Berries, 1 pint = 2 cups
Cantaloupe, 2 pounds, 1 average =
    3 cups, diced

Cherries, 1 pint = 1 cup, pitted
Cranberries, 1 pound = 4-1/2 cups
Crenshaw melon, 3 pounds, 1 average =
    4-1/2 cups, diced
Figs, 1 pound, 4 small = 2 cups,
    chopped
Grapefruit, 1 small = 1 cup, sectioned
Grapes, Concord, 1/4 pound,
    30 grapes = 1 cup
Grapes, Thompson seedless, 1/4 pound,
    40 grapes = 1 cup
Guavas, 1 pound, 4 medium = 1 cup,
    chopped
Honeydew melon, 2 pounds, 1 average
    = 3 cups, diced
Kumquats, 1 pound, 8 to 10 average =
    2 cups, sliced
Lemon, 1 medium (3 average =
    1 pound) = 3 tablespoons juice;
    2 teaspoons grated peel
Limes, 1/2 pound, 5 average =
    4 tablespoons juice; 4 to 5
    teaspoons grated peel
Loquats, 1 pound, 5 average =
    1-1/2 cups, chopped
Lychees, 1 pound, 6 average = 1/2 cup,
    chopped
Mangoes, 1 pound, 2 average = 1-1/2
    cups, chopped
Nectarines, 1 pound, 3 average =
    2 cups, chopped
Orange, 1 small (2 average = 1 pound)
    = 6 tablespoons juice; 1 tablespoon
    grated peel, 3/4 cup, sectioned
Papaya, 1 medium = 1-1/2 cups,
    chopped

Peaches, 1 pound, 3 average = 2 cups,
chopped

Pears, 1 pound, 3 average = 2 cups,
chopped

Persimmons, 1 pound, 3 average =
2 cups, mashed

Pineapple, 3 pounds, 1 medium =
2-1/2 cups, chopped

Plums, 1 pound, 4 average = 2 cups,
chopped

Pomegranate, 1/4 pound, 1 average =
3 cups seeds

Prunes, 1 pound, 5 average = 2 cups,
chopped

Rhubarb, 1 pound, 4 slender stalks =
2 cups, cooked

Tangerines, 1 pound, 4 average =
2 cups, sectioned

Watermelon, 10 to 12 pounds,
1 average = 20 to 24 cups, cubed

HERBS, SPICES AND SEASONINGS

Garlic powder, 1/8 teaspoon = 1 small
clove garlic

Ginger, powdered, 1/2 teaspoon =
1 teaspoon, fresh

Herbs, dried, 1/2 teaspoon = 1 tablespoon, fresh

Horseradish, bottled, 2 tablespoons =
1 tablespoon, fresh

MILK

Dry, whole powdered milk, 1/4 cup +
1 cup water = 1 cup whole milk

Dry, instant non-fat powdered milk,
1/3 cup + 2/3 cup water = 1 cup
non-fat milk

Dry, non-instant non-fat powdered
milk, 3 tablespoons + 1 cup water =
1 cup non-fat milk

Skimmed, canned, 1 cup = 5 cups,
whipped

PROTEIN

Cheese

Cottage cheese, 1/2 pound = 1 cup

Cheese, grated, 1/4 pound = 1 cup

Chicken

Chicken, 3-1/2 pound, roasted, boned
and skinned = 3 cups, chopped

Eggs and Egg Substitutes

Eggs, raw, in shell, 10 medium =
1 pound

Egg whites, 1 medium = 1-1/2
tablespoons

Egg whites, 9 medium = 1 cup

Egg yolks, 1 medium = 1 tablespoon

Egg yolks, 16 medium = 1 cup

Egg, hard-cooked, 1 = 1/3 cup,
finely chopped

Egg substitute, liquid, 1/4 cup =
1 egg (see label)

Egg substitute, dry, 3 tablespoons =
1 egg (see label)

Seafood and Fish

Crab, fresh or frozen, cooked or
canned, 1/2 pound (5-1/2- to
7-1/2-ounce tin) = 1 cup

Escargots, 6 = 1-1/2 ounces

Lobster, fresh or frozen, cooked,
1/2 pound = 1 cup

Oysters, raw, 1/2 pound = 1 cup

Scallops, fresh or frozen, shucked,
1/2 pound = 1 cup

Shrimp, cooked, 1 pound = 3 cups

Tuna, drained, canned, 6-1/2 to
7 ounces = 3/4 cup

STARCHES

Crumbs

Bread crumbs, soft, 1 slice = 3/4 cup

Bread crumbs, dry, crumbled, 2 slices
= 1/2 cup

Bread crumbs, dry, ground, 4 slices =
1/2 cup

Graham crackers, 14 squares, fine
crumbs = 1 cup

Soda crackers, 21 squares, fine crumbs
= 1 cup

Cereals and Noodles

Flour, cake, 1 pound = 4-1/2 cups,
sifted

Flour, all-purpose, 1 pound = 4 cups

Bulgur, 1/3 cup = 1 cup, cooked

Cornmeal, 1 cup = 4 cups, cooked

Macaroni, 1 pound, 5 cups = 12 cups,
cooked

Noodles, 1 pound, 5-1/2 cups = 10
cups, cooked

Oatmeal, quick-cooking, 1 cup =
2 cups, cooked

Spaghetti, 1 pound = 9 cups, cooked

STOCK BASE AND
BOUILLON CUBES

Beef Stock Base, Powdered

1 teaspoon = 1 bouillon cube

4 teaspoons + 1-1/4 cups water =
1 10-1/2-ounce can bouillon,
undiluted

1 teaspoon + 5 ounces water = 5
ounces stock

1 teaspoon + 1 cup water = 1 cup
bouillon

Chicken Stock Base, Powdered

1 teaspoon = 1 bouillon cube

1 teaspoon + 5 ounces water = 5
ounces stock

1 teaspoon + 1 cup water = 1 cup
bouillon

VEGETABLES (DRIED)
Garbanzo beans, 1 pound, 2 cups =
   6 cups, cooked
Kidney beans, 1 pound, 1-1/2 cups =
   9 cups, cooked
Lima or navy beans, 1 pound,
   2-1/2 cups = 6 cups, cooked
Rice, 1 pound, 2-1/2 cups = 8 cups,
   cooked
Split peas, 1 pound, 2 cups = 5 cups,
   cooked

VEGETABLES (FRESH)
Artichokes, 1/2 pound = 1 average
Asparagus, 1 pound, 18 spears =
   2 cups, cut in 1-inch pieces
Avocado, 1 medium = 2 cups, chopped
Beans, green, 1 pound = 3 cups,
   chopped and cooked
Beets, 1 pound, medium-size = 2 cups,
   cooked and sliced
Bell pepper, 1/2 pound, 1 large = 1 cup,
   seeded and finely chopped
Broccoli, 1 pound, 2 stalks = 6 cups,
   chopped and cooked
Brussels sprouts, 1 pound, 28 average =
   4 cups
Cabbage, 1 pound = 4 cups, shredded;
   2-1/2 cups, cooked
Carrots, 1 pound, 8 small = 4 cups,
   chopped
Cauliflower, 1-1/2 pounds, 1 average =
   6 cups, chopped and cooked
Celery, 1 stalk = 1/2 cup, finely
   chopped
Celery root, 1-3/4 pounds, 1 average =
   4 cups raw, grated; 2 cups, cooked
   and mashed

Corn, 6 ears = 1-1/2 cups, cut
Cucumber, 1 medium = 1-1/2 cups,
   sliced
Eggplant, 1 pound, 1 medium =
   12 1/4-inch slices; 6 cups, cubed
Lettuce, 1 average head = 6 cups, bite-
   size pieces
Lima beans, baby, 1 pound = 2 cups
Mushrooms, fresh, 1/2 pound, 20
   medium = 2 cups raw, sliced
Okra, 24 medium = 1/2 pound
Onion, 1 medium = 1 cup, finely
   chopped
Parsnips, 1 pound, 6 average = 4 cups,
   chopped
Peas, in pods, 1 pound = 1 cup, shelled
   and cooked
Pimiento, 1 4-ounce jar = 1/2 cup,
   chopped
Potatoes, 1 pound, 4 medium =
   2-1/2 cups, cooked and diced
Pumpkin, 3 pounds, 1 average piece =
   4 cups, cooked and mashed
Rutabagas, 1-1/2 pounds, 3 small =
   2 cups, cooked and mashed
Spinach, 1 pound = 3-1/2 cups,
   uncooked; 1 cup, cooked
Squash, acorn, 1-1/2 pounds, 1 average
   = 2 cups, cooked and mashed
Squash, banana, 3 pounds, 1 average
   piece = 4 cups, cooked and mashed
Squash, summer, 1 pound, 4 average =
   1 cup, cooked
Squash, zucchini, 1 pound, 2 average
   = 1-1/4 cups, cooked and chopped;
   3 cups raw, diced

Tomatoes, 1 pound, 3 medium =
   1-1/4 cups, cooked and chopped
Turnips, white, 1 pound, 3 small =
   2 cups, peeled and grated;
   1-1/4 cups, cooked and mashed

MISCELLANEOUS
Chocolate, 1 square, 1 ounce =
   4 tablespoons, grated
Gelatin, sheet, 4 sheets = 1 envelope
Gelatin, powdered, 1/4-ounce
   envelope = 1 scant tablespoon
Yeast, fresh, 1 package = 2 tablespoons
Yeast, dry, 1 envelope (to be recon-
   stituted in 2 tablespoons water) =
   1-3/4 tablespoons

METRIC WEIGHTS
For Dry Measure
Convert known ounces into grams by
   multiplying by 28
Convert known pounds into kilograms
   by multiplying by .45
Convert known grams into ounces by
   multiplying by .035
Convert known kilograms into pounds
   by multiplying by 2.2
For Liquid Measure
Convert known ounces into milliliters
   by multiplying by 30
Convert known pints into liters by
   multiplying by .47
Convert known quarts into liters by
   multiplying by .95
Convert known gallons into liters by
   multiplying by 3.8
Convert known milliliters into ounces
   by multiplying by .034

bibliography

American Heart Association. *Mild Sodium Restricted Diet.* New York: American Heart Association, 1969.

American Heart Association. *Your 500 Milligram Sodium Diet.* New York: American Heart Association, 1968.

American Heart Association. *Your 1000 Milligram Sodium Diet.* New York: American Heart Association, 1969.

Bagg, Elma W. *Cooking Without A Grain of Salt.* New York: Doubleday & Company, Inc., 1964.

Bowes & Church. *Food Values of Portions Commonly Used,* 12th ed. Philadelphia: J. B. Lippincott Company, 1975.

Bringas, Juliet G., and Chan, Teresa Y. *1000 Milligrams Sodium Diet.* Los Angeles: Nutrition in the Life Cycle, 1977.

Bringas, Juliet G., and Chan, Teresa Y. *The Sodium Restricted Diabetic Diet.* Los Angeles: Nutrition in the Life Cycle, 1977.

Bringas, Juliet G., and Chan, Teresa Y. *Two Gram Sodium Diet.* Los Angeles: Nutrition in the Life Cycle, 1978.

Conason, Emil G., M.D., and Metz, Ella. *The Salt-Free Diet Cook Book.* New York: Grosset & Dunlap, 1969.

Johnston, Barbara, and Koh, Maria. *Halt! No Salt.* Bellevue, Washington: Dietary Research, 1974.

Jones, Jeanne. *The Calculating Cook.* San Francisco: 101 Productions, 1978.

Jones, Jeanne. *Diet for a Happy Heart.* San Francisco: 101 Productions, 1975.

Jones, Jeanne. *Fabulous Fiber Cookbook.* San Francisco. 101 Productions, 1977.

Kraus, Barbara. *The Dictionary of Sodium, Fats, and Cholesterol.* New York: Grosset & Dunlap, 1977.

Leonard, Jon N.; Hofer, J. L.; and Pritikin, N. *Live Longer Now.* New York: Grosset & Dunlap, 1974.

Mayer, Jean, M.D. *A Diet for Living.* New York: Pocket Books, 1977. (David McKay, 1975.)

Payne, Alma Smith, and Callahan, Dorothy. *The Fat and Sodium Control Cookbook.* Boston: Little, Brown and Company, 1965.

Thorburn, Anna Houston, with Turner, Phyllis. *Living Salt Free & Easy.* New York: Signet, 1976.

United States Department of Agriculture. "Composition of Foods—Raw, Processed, Prepared." *Revised U.S.D.A. Agricultural Handbook,* Number 8, 1975.

United States Department of Agriculture. "Nutritive Value of American Foods in Common Units." *U.S.D.A. Agricultural Handbook,* Number 456, 1975.

index

biographical notes

JEANNE JONES

Jeanne Jones is internationally recognized as one of the leading writers and lecturers in the diet field. Her three cookbooks, *The Calculating Cook, Diet for a Happy Heart* and *Fabulous Fiber Cookbook,* have been widely acclaimed and are often prescribed by doctors and dietitians. She also serves as a consultant on recipe development and menu planning for a number of health organizations, diet-food manufacturers and restaurants. She has lectured here and abroad at professional meetings of nutritionists, and has appeared as a guest expert on diet and cooking on nearly 100 radio and television programs throughout the United States and Cananda.

Jeanne Jones' serious interest in nutrition began when she was placed on a diabetic diet and realized that this diet was not as restrictive as it first appeared but rather just a perfectly balanced diet. Refusing to relinquish her role as a gourmet cook and hostess, she used her international background in foods and entertaining to create a unique approach to recipes and menus for others on restricted diets. The recipes became the basis for her book *The Calculating Cook: A Gourmet Cookbook for Diabetics and Dieters,* published in 1972. The book subsequently was approved for use by diabetics by the American Diabetes Association and was named the best adult book of the year by the National Federation of Press Women. Over 150,000 copies have been sold to date.

For her second book, *Diet for a Happy Heart,* Jeanne Jones developed a collection of recipes low in cholesterol, low in saturated fat and sugar free. Published in 1975, *Happy Heart* has sold over 75,000 copies. This was followed in 1977 by the publication of the *Fabulous Fiber Cookbook,* which was also published in England.

Jeanne Jones is an editorial associate of *Diabetes Forecast,* the official magazine of the American Diabetes Association, and a member of the External Advisory Committee to the Diet Modification Program of the National Heart and Blood Vessel Research Demonstration Center in Houston. She serves on the boards of directors of the San Diego County Heart Association; the Southern California Affiliate of the American Diabetes Association; and the San Diego Chapter of the American Diabetes Association. In 1976, she was chairman of a diet panel for the International Diabetes Federation Congress in New Delhi.

KAREN OKASAKI SASAKI

A free-lance illustrator and designer, Karen Okasaki Sasaki received her bachelor's degree in fine arts from the University of California at Davis. She later studied illustration for two years at Art Center College of Design in Los Angeles. She has also illustrated *The Book of Yogurt* for 101 Productions.